Tying The Knot

A Stress-Free Guide to Your Perfect Day

By Ange Antony

Tying the Knot

Ange Antony

Published by Ange Antony, 2024.

TYING THE KNOT

First edition. May 12, 2024.

ISBN: 979-8224472055

Written by Ange Antony.

To my beloved family,

Thank you for your unwavering love, support, and encouragement throughout this journey. Your endless belief in me has been my guiding light. This book is dedicated to you, for your boundless love and for being the heartbeat of my world.

With all my love and gratitude

Introduction

L et's bring your vision to life!

THIS IS AN ESSENTIAL guide that every bride must have for crafting the perfect wedding day. A wedding can feel overwhelming at times, but fear not! We're here to guide you through the process with expert tips, friendly advice, and a touch of magic.

Planning a dream wedding doesn't have to come with a hefty price tag. In this guide we will explore the compelling reasons why more and more couples are opting to take the reins themselves, steering clear of expensive wedding planners. With this trusty guide in your hands, you're about to embark on the empowering journey of becoming your very own wedding architect. Get ready to roll up your sleeves, unleash your creativity, and craft the wedding day of your dreams like a seasoned pro!

This guide is crafted with insights from wedding experts, offering a wealth of knowledge covering every aspect of wedding planning. It's like having a seasoned wedding planner by your side, ensuring no detail is overlooked. Focused on practical advice, the guide provides clear dos and don'ts, steering brides away from common pitfalls and offering actionable steps to navigate the complexities of wedding planning. Rooted in timeless principles, the guide provides enduring wisdom that remains relevant regardless of changing trends. It's a dependable resource that withstands the test of time, offering guidance that is as valuable today as it will be in the future. Recognizing the diversity of wedding traditions, the guide embraces cultural sensitivity. It helps brides navigate the nuances of various customs, ensuring inclusivity and respect for different cultural practices.

The guide empowers brides to make informed decisions, encouraging them to infuse their personalities into the planning process. It's not just about creating a perfect day; it's all about crafting a day that reflects your unique love story. Wedding planning can be overwhelming, but this guide equips brides with stress-reduction strategies. From practical timelines to relaxation tips, it ensures that the journey to the altar is as enjoyable and stress-free as possible. Packed with creative inspiration, the guide sparks ideas for personalizing the wedding. Whether it's décor, themes, or unique touches, brides will find a trove of inspiration to make their day truly one-of-a-kind.

Recognizing the importance of financial considerations, you will find budget-friendly tips that won't compromise the day's magic. It's a practical resource for brides looking to maximize their budget while creating a memorable celebration. Featuring comprehensive checklists and curated resources, the guide streamlines the planning process. Brides can stay organized, ticking off tasks confidently and ensuring every detail is noticed. Above all, the guide advocates for a joyful celebration. It encourages brides to focus on the love they share with their partner and relish the moments leading up to the wedding day. It's not just about the event; it's about savoring the entire journey.

In essence, this guide is a trusted ally, offering a blend of expertise, practical advice, and creative inspiration to ensure that every bride feels empowered and excited as she navigates the path to her perfect wedding day.

So, cozy up, and let's dive into a world where wedding planning is not just about to-do lists and deadlines, but a delightful journey filled with excitement and joy. "Tying The Knot" is your companion on this adventure, ensuring that your path to the perfect day is not just stress-free but also filled with wonder and awe. Get ready to say "I do" to a wedding experience that exceeds your expectations!

Crafting a stress-free wedding requires insight, experience, and a passion for ensuring couples embark on their journey to marital bliss with ease. As the author of this guide, I bring a unique blend of expertise and knowledge that stems from years of research and experience.

Please refer to and utilize the online budgeting apps and additional digital tools mentioned towards the end of this book to help plan your wedding. These resources are invaluable for staying organized, managing expenses, and ensuring that every aspect of your special day is well-coordinated and executed smoothly. Whether you're tracking your budget, managing your guest list, or organizing your wedding timeline, these digital tools can streamline the planning process and make your wedding journey more efficient and enjoyable.

Chapter 1

Setting the tone for a stress-free wedding journey

CONGRATULATIONS ON your engagement! As you begin this exciting chapter of your life, it's natural to feel a whirlwind of emotions—from excitement and anticipation to a touch of apprehension about the wedding planning process. In this chapter, we'll explore how to set the tone for a stress-free wedding journey, ensuring that your path to the altar is as smooth and enjoyable as possible. The ultimate must-have guide to planning a stress-free, wedding day! Welcome to "Tying the Knot, A Stress-Free Guide to Your Perfect Day"! We're thrilled to embark on this delightful journey with you as we unravel the secrets to planning your dream wedding day.

Imagine your dream wedding – a day filled with love, laughter, and cherished moments. Now, envision achieving that vision without the stress that often comes with wedding planning. That's precisely what you're about to discover how to achieve.

In this introductory chapter, we're setting the stage for a stress-free wedding journey. I have gained extensive knowledge by delving into the intricacies of wedding planning, understanding the challenges couples face, and discovering effective strategies to overcome them. This hands-on experience provides valuable insights into the nuances of orchestrating a seamless celebration. My expertise is grounded in thorough research of wedding planning trends, industry best practices, and the latest developments.

Remaining attuned to the ever-changing wedding scene ensures that the guidance offered is not only timeless but also mirrors the latest trends and advancements. Recognizing that weddings are deeply rooted in cultural traditions, I've delved into various customs and practices to provide inclusive and culturally sensitive guidance. Navigating the diverse landscape of wedding traditions allows for a comprehensive and respectful approach to planning. Interactions with seasoned wedding professionals, including planners, photographers, florists, and caterers, have enriched my understanding of the collaborative efforts required to execute a flawless event. Drawing from their expertise adds depth to the dos and don'ts shared in this guide.

I approach wedding planning with a genuine understanding of the emotional significance of the occasion. By empathizing with the dreams, concerns, and aspirations of couples, I aim to provide guidance that goes beyond logistics, fostering a more personal and meaningful wedding experience. The wedding industry evolves, and trends shift. By maintaining a commitment to continuous learning and adaptability, I ensure that the advice offered is not only relevant today but also adaptable to the evolving landscape of weddings. My passion lies in creating stress-free celebrations that allow couples to fully savor the joy of their special day. The dos and don'ts presented in this guide are rooted in the belief that weddings should be moments of pure happiness, and meticulous planning can contribute significantly to achieving this vision.

By embracing these principles, you'll create a joyful and memorable experience leading up to your big day.

Clarifying Your Priorities

Reflecting on What Matters Most: Take some time to reflect on your values, dreams, and priorities as a couple. What do you envision for your wedding day, and what aspects are most important to you? By clarifying your priorities early on, you can focus your energy on the elements that truly matter and let go of unnecessary stressors.

Establishing Open Communication

Candid Conversations: Foster open and honest communication with your partner about your hopes, concerns, and expectations for the wedding. Discuss your individual preferences, budget considerations, and any potential challenges you anticipate. Building a strong foundation of communication will help you navigate decisions together and support each other throughout the planning process.

Creating a Realistic Timeline

Setting Milestones: Break down the wedding planning process into manageable steps and create a realistic timeline to guide your progress. Start with big-picture tasks like choosing a date and venue, then gradually move on to details like selecting vendors and finalizing decor. By pacing yourself and setting achievable milestones, you'll avoid feeling overwhelmed and stay on track for a stress-free journey.

Practicing Self-Care

Prioritizing Well-Being: Make self-care a priority as you navigate the demands of wedding planning. Schedule regular breaks, practice mindfulness or meditation in your daily routine, and engage in activities that bring you joy and relaxation. Whether it's through meditation, deep breathing exercises, or yoga, take time to center yourself and find moments of calm amidst the busyness of wedding planning. Taking care of your physical, mental, and emotional well-being will help you stay grounded and resilient in the face of challenges.

Delegate and Share Responsibilities

Enlisting Help: Don't hesitate to reach out to friends, family members, or professional wedding planners for support and assistance. Delegate tasks where possible and lean on your support network for guidance, advice, and encouragement. Remember, you don't have to do it all alone, and asking for help is a sign of strength, not weakness. Working together as a team will lighten the load and make the planning process more enjoyable for everyone involved.

Maintaining Flexibility and Adaptability

Embracing Imperfection: Accept that not everything will go according to plan, and that's okay! Embrace the beauty of imperfection and be willing to adapt to unforeseen circumstances with grace and flexibility. Your wedding day is about celebrating your love and commitment, and the most important thing is the journey you share with your partner.

Embrace Positivity and Optimism

Cultivate a positive mindset and approach your wedding planning journey with optimism. Focus on the joy and excitement of marrying the love of your life, rather than getting bogged down by stress or anxiety.

Stay Organized and Prepared

Invest in organizational tools such as planners, calendars, or digital apps to keep track of deadlines, appointments, and tasks. Being prepared and staying on top of your to-do list will help you feel more in control and less overwhelmed.

Set Boundaries and Manage Expectations

Establish clear boundaries with well-meaning friends and family members to prevent overwhelm and maintain focus on your vision for the wedding. Communicate your needs and priorities openly, and don't hesitate to say no to requests or suggestions that don't align with your vision.

Celebrate Milestones and Achievements

Take time to celebrate milestones and achievements along the way, whether it's securing a venue, finding the perfect dress, or finalizing your guest list. Recognize and appreciate the progress you've made, and savor the moments of joy and accomplishment.

As you embark on this remarkable journey of wedding planning, remember that the tone you set from the beginning will shape your experience every step of the way. By clarifying your priorities, fostering open communication, creating a realistic timeline, practicing self-care, seeking support, and maintaining flexibility, you can lay the foundation for a stress-free and enjoyable wedding journey.

Whether you're just beginning to envision your dream wedding or finalizing the last details, this guide is here to support you every step of the way, ensuring that your wedding planning experience is not only stress-free but also enjoyable and memorable.

10 REASONS THAT MAKE this guide stand out

1. *The Power of Personalization*

Why Settle for Cookie-Cutter when you can unleash your creativity and infuse your personality into every detail? Learn how a DIY approach allows you to tailor every aspect of your wedding to reflect your unique love story.

2. *Budget Bliss*

Delve into the financial benefits of a DIY wedding. Discover practical tips and tricks to stretch your budget further, allowing you to allocate funds to what truly matters to you.

3. *Timelines on Your Terms*

Explore the freedom of setting your own timelines. From booking venues to sending invitations, understand how DIY planning lets you pace the journey according to your preferences.

4. *Vendor Negotiation Know-How*

Learn valuable negotiation skills to secure the best deals from vendors. This chapter arms you with the knowledge to navigate vendor contracts and get the most out of your budget.

5. *DIY Décor Delights*

Crafting Memories, not Expenses as you dive into the world of DIY décor. From centerpieces to signage, discover creative and budget-friendly ways to adorn your celebration with personalized touches.

6. *Stress-Free Decision-Making*

Explore the emotional benefits of hands-on planning. By making decisions yourself, you'll find a sense of satisfaction and joy that comes from creating a day that truly represents you as a couple.

7. *Building a Support Network*

Learn how involving friends and family can turn the wedding planning process into a bonding experience. Build a support network that enhances the joy of preparing for your big day.

8. The Digital Advantage

Embrace the digital tools and resources available. From online planning platforms to budgeting apps, discover how technology can streamline the planning process, making it both efficient and enjoyable.

9. Problem-Solving Prowess

Equip yourself with problem-solving skills. Learn how to navigate unexpected challenges with confidence, turning potential pitfalls into opportunities for creative solutions.

10. The Satisfaction of Success

Explore the sense of accomplishment that comes with pulling off a DIY wedding. From the initial planning stages to the last dance, savor the satisfaction of seeing your vision come to life.

By the end of this book, you'll understand why investing in a wedding planner isn't the only path to a spectacular celebration. Discover the joy, empowerment, and financial freedom that come with being your own wedding maestro, guided by this trusty DIY handbook.

Chapter 2

Crafting Your Wedding Vision

WELCOME TO THE HEART of your wedding planning journey – In this chapter, we'll unravel the art of crafting a realistic timeline and by carefully selecting services that align with your vision, budget, and priorities, you can create a wedding day that reflects your unique style and personality while ensuring a memorable and seamless experience for you and your guests.

Imagine your wedding plans falling seamlessly into place, like a perfectly choreographed dance. To achieve this, the first step is creating a realistic timeline. Start by outlining key milestones, from choosing the venue to sending out invitations. Break down larger tasks into manageable steps, setting deadlines for each. For instance, three months before the big day, aim to finalize your guest list, and six months ahead, focus on selecting your dream dress or suit. By having a well-structured timeline, you'll feel in control, organized, and ready to tackle each task with ease.

A realistic timeline with thoughtful planning will contribute to the canvas of your dream day. As you start this journey, immerse yourself in the joy of ticking off each milestone. From choosing the venue that resonates with your love story to picking out the perfect invitations that capture the essence of your celebration – every task completed is a step forward, bringing you closer to the wedding day crescendo.

Embarking on the journey of wedding planning is an exciting time filled with anticipation, dreams, and endless possibilities. In this chapter, we'll dive into the foundational steps of crafting your wedding vision by setting the date and establishing a budget. These crucial decisions will shape the direction of your wedding planning process and lay the groundwork for bringing your vision to life.

Setting the Date:

Considerations and Factors: Discuss the various factors to consider when selecting your wedding date, including seasonality, availability of venues and vendors, personal significance (such as anniversaries or meaningful dates), and potential conflicts or considerations for guests.

Flexibility and Priorities: Encourage couples to remain flexible and open-minded when choosing a wedding date, especially if certain factors are non-negotiable (such as a specific venue or vendor availability). Emphasize the importance of prioritizing what matters most to the couple in terms of timing and logistics.

Research and Planning: Offer tips for conducting research and planning ahead when selecting a wedding date, including reaching out to venues and vendors early, exploring potential date options, and considering any external factors or events that may impact availability or pricing.

Establishing Your Budget:

Financial Considerations: Discuss the importance of establishing a realistic wedding budget based on the couple's financial resources, priorities, and desired level of investment in their wedding day. Encourage open and honest discussions about finances and expectations to ensure alignment and agreement between partners.

Budget Allocation: budget categories based on the couple's priorities and preferences, including venue, catering, attire, decor, entertainment, photography, and other expenses. Offer general guidelines or percentages for each category to help couples allocate their budget effectively.

Contingency Planning: Stress the importance of budgeting for unexpected expenses or emergencies by setting aside a contingency fund or buffer. Discuss strategies for managing costs, negotiating with vendors, and making informed decisions to stay within budget while still achieving the couple's vision for their wedding day.

Setting the date and establishing a budget are the first steps in bringing your wedding vision to life. By carefully considering factors such as timing, availability, and financial resources, couples can lay a strong foundation for the planning process and make informed decisions that align with their priorities and goals. As you embark on this journey together, remember that your wedding day is a celebration of your love and commitment, and with careful planning and thoughtful decision-making, it will be a day to remember for a lifetime.

Before the big day arrives, several pre-wedding events provide opportunities for couples to celebrate their love with family and friends. Before the excitement of the wedding day takes center stage, there are special pre-wedding events that allow couples to share their joy and anticipation with loved ones. In this chapter, we'll explore the significance of engagement parties, bridal showers, and rehearsal dinners, offering valuable insights and tips for planning and hosting these memorable celebrations.

Engagement Parties: Celebrating the Start of Forever

Setting the Tone: An engagement party marks the official beginning of the wedding festivities and provides an opportunity for friends and family to congratulate the couple.

Choosing the Venue: Consider hosting the party at a meaningful location, such as a favorite restaurant, backyard garden, or cozy home setting.

Guest List Etiquette: Keep the guest list manageable and inclusive, inviting close family members, friends, and those who will play a significant role in the wedding.

Personal Touches: Incorporate personal touches that reflect the couple's style and personalities, such as themed decorations, custom cocktails, or heartfelt speeches.

Bridal Showers: Showering the Bride-to-Be with Love

Honoring the Bride: A bridal shower is a special occasion to celebrate the bride-to-be and shower her with love, gifts, and well wishes.

Planning Considerations: Coordinate with the bridal party or close family members to plan the shower, taking into account the bride's preferences and interests.

Themes and Activities: Choose a theme or concept that reflects the bride's personality, whether it's a spa day, garden party, or brunch gathering. Plan fun activities and games to keep guests entertained and engaged.

Gift Etiquette: Provide guidance to guests on gift preferences and registry information, ensuring that gifts are thoughtful and practical for the bride's upcoming journey into marriage.

Rehearsal Dinners: Setting the Stage for the Wedding Day

Gathering Loved Ones: The rehearsal dinner brings together key members of the wedding party, including close family and friends, to rehearse the ceremony and enjoy an intimate meal together.

Venue Selection: Choose a venue that complements the wedding theme and offers a relaxed and inviting atmosphere for guests to mingle and connect.

Speeches and Toasts: Incorporate speeches and toasts to express gratitude, share memories, and offer words of encouragement for the couple's future.

Culinary Delights: Select a menu that showcases the couple's favorite dishes or highlights local cuisine, providing guests with a memorable dining experience.

Pre-wedding celebrations offer valuable opportunities for couples to gather with loved ones and create lasting memories before the big day. By carefully planning and hosting engagement parties, bridal showers, and rehearsal dinners, couples can set the stage for a wedding celebration filled with love, laughter, and cherished moments.

Host Responsibilities: Discuss the responsibilities of the hosts (typically the groom's parents) in hosting the rehearsal dinner, including managing the guest list, making reservations, and overseeing the event's logistics. Offer suggestions for incorporating personal touches and meaningful elements into the dinner to make it a memorable occasion for all.

When it comes to planning a wedding, there are several best practices to follow and potential pitfalls to avoid. Here are some key points to consider:

Best Practices:

Start planning early: Begin your wedding preparations well in advance to avoid last-minute stress and ensure you have enough time to make all necessary arrangements.

Set a realistic budget: Determine your budget early on and allocate funds to different aspects of the wedding, such as venue, catering, attire, and decorations.

Prioritize your needs: Identify the most important elements of your wedding and allocate a larger portion of your budget to them. This will help ensure that you get the most out of your money.

Research vendors: Take the time to research and vet potential vendors, such as caterers, florists, photographers, and DJs. Look for reputable professionals with positive reviews and a portfolio of work that aligns with your vision.

Communicate openly: Maintain clear and open communication with your partner, family, and vendors throughout the planning process. This will help prevent misunderstandings and ensure that everyone is on the same page.

Stay organized: Keep track of important dates, deadlines, and details using a wedding planning checklist or organizer. This will help you stay organized and ensure that nothing falls through the cracks.

Be flexible: Understand that not everything will go according to plan, and be prepared to adapt to unexpected changes or challenges. A flexible attitude will help you navigate any obstacles that arise with grace and ease.

Potential Pitfalls to Avoid:

Overcommitting your budget: Avoid overspending by sticking to your budget and resisting the temptation to splurge on unnecessary extras.

Ignoring contract details: Read and understand all vendor contracts thoroughly before signing to avoid any surprises or disputes later on.

Procrastinating on tasks: Don't leave important tasks until the last minute, as this can lead to unnecessary stress and rushed decisions.

Neglecting self-care: Remember to take care of yourself amidst the wedding planning process by prioritizing rest, relaxation, and self-care activities.

Allowing others to dictate your decisions: While it's important to consider the opinions of loved ones, ultimately, the wedding should reflect your preferences and values. Don't feel pressured to conform to others' expectations.

Failing to communicate boundaries: Be clear about your boundaries and expectations with family, friends, and vendors to avoid misunderstandings and conflicts.

Sweating the small stuff: Keep things in perspective and don't let minor details overshadow the joy and significance of the occasion. Focus on what truly matters: celebrating your love and commitment to each other.

Wedding suppliers

Also known as a wedding vendor or service provider, is a business or individual that offers products or services specifically tailored to weddings. These suppliers play a crucial role in helping couples bring their wedding vision to life by providing everything from venue rentals and catering to floral arrangements, photography, entertainment, and more. Some common types of wedding suppliers include:

Venues: These are locations where wedding ceremonies and receptions take place, such as banquet halls, hotels, gardens, vineyards, and historic landmarks.

Caterers: Catering companies provide food and beverage services for weddings, ranging from full-course meals and buffets to cocktail receptions and dessert bars.

Florists: Florists specialize in creating floral arrangements for weddings, including bouquets, centerpieces, boutonnieres, and ceremony decor.

Photographers/Videographers: These professionals capture the special moments of the wedding day through photography and videography, providing couples with lasting memories of their celebration.

Entertainment: This category includes DJs, bands, musicians, and other performers who provide music and entertainment for the wedding ceremony, cocktail hour, and reception.

Wedding Planners/Coordinators: Wedding planners offer comprehensive planning services to help couples manage every aspect of their wedding, while coordinators provide day-of coordination to ensure that the event runs smoothly.

Stationery Designers: Stationery designers create wedding invitations, save-the-dates, programs, and other paper goods that set the tone for the wedding and provide important information to guests.

Cake Designers/Bakers: Cake designers and bakers specialize in creating custom wedding cakes and desserts that reflect the couple's tastes and wedding theme.

Rental Companies: Rental companies supply furniture, decor, linens, tableware, and other items needed to furnish and decorate the wedding venue.

Hair and Makeup Artists: These professionals provide hair styling and makeup services for the bride, bridal party, and other members of the wedding party.

These are just a few examples of the many types of wedding suppliers available to couples as they plan their special day. Each supplier plays a vital role in bringing the wedding vision to life and ensuring that the celebration is memorable and seamless for the couple and their guests.

Building a team of skilled professionals who will contribute to the seamless execution of your wedding day is essential to a seamless wedding day. By following the dos and steering clear of the pitfalls, you'll assemble a dream team that turns your wedding vision into a reality.

Do: Researching and Selecting Top-Notch Suppliers

Start Early - Initiate your supplier search well in advance

Early bookings secure the best vendors and give you ample time for thorough research

Tap into Recommendations: Seek recommendations from friends, family, or recently married couples

Online reviews and testimonials provide valuable insights into a supplier's reputation

Research Portfolios - Carefully review the portfolios of photographers, videographers, and other visual suppliers. Ensure their style aligns with your vision for the day.

Meet Potential Suppliers - Schedule meetings or consultations with your shortlisted suppliers. Gauge their professionalism, communication style, and enthusiasm for your wedding.

Clarify Terms and Contracts - Request detailed quotes and contracts from each supplier

Clarify payment terms, cancellation policies, and any other crucial details.

Don't: Falling into Supplier Pitfalls

Ignoring Reviews - Don't disregard online reviews or testimonials. Negative feedback can be insightful, and positive reviews validate a supplier's reliability.

Neglecting Clear Communication - Avoid suppliers who are unclear or unresponsive in their communication.

Clear communication is key to a smooth collaboration.

Overlooking Flexibility - Ensure your suppliers are flexible and can adapt to unforeseen circumstances. The rigidity can lead to challenges on the wedding day.

Not Confirming Backup Plans - Inquire about backup plans for outdoor suppliers in case of inclement weather. Ensure your suppliers have contingency measures in place.

Don't be afraid to ask questions and request samples or portfolios to get a better sense of each supplier's style and capabilities. A simple checklist on how to thoroughly assess potential suppliers for your wedding involves asking the right questions and conducting thorough research. Here are some key steps and questions to consider:

Research: Start by researching potential suppliers online. Look for reviews, testimonials, and examples of their work. Check their website and social media pages to get a sense of their style and professionalism.

Availability: Determine if the supplier is available on your wedding date. If not, there's no need to proceed further.

Experience: Ask about the supplier's experience in the wedding industry. How long have they been in business? How many weddings have they worked on? Do they have experience with weddings similar to yours in size and style?

Portfolio: Request to see examples of their previous work. This could include photos of past weddings, videos, or samples of their products (e.g., invitations, and floral arrangements).

References: Ask for references from past clients. Contact these references to inquire about their experience working with the supplier and if they would recommend them.

Services: Clarify what services the supplier provides. For example, if you're hiring a wedding planner, what specific tasks will they handle? If you're booking a photographer, what's included in their packages?

Cost and Payment: Discuss pricing upfront. What are their rates or package options? Are there any additional fees or hidden costs? What is their payment schedule?

Contracts: Review the supplier's contract carefully. What are their cancellation and refund policies? Are there any clauses or terms you're uncomfortable with?

Communication: Assess their communication style and responsiveness. Are they prompt and professional in their replies? Do they listen to your concerns and preferences?

Flexibility and Creativity: Inquire about their flexibility and ability to accommodate your specific needs and preferences. Are they open to customizing their services or packages?

Backup Plans: Ask about their contingency plans in case of emergencies or unforeseen circumstances. For example, what happens if they fall ill or encounter technical issues?

Insurance and Licenses: Ensure that the supplier has the necessary insurance coverage and licenses to operate legally. This is especially important for vendors like caterers and transportation providers.

By being diligent and deliberate in your selection process, you can ensure that you're making informed decisions that align with your vision and budget for your wedding. Remember, it's better to take your time and choose the right suppliers than to rush and end up disappointed on your wedding day.

WEDDING PLANNING TIMELINES- A Blueprint for Your Perfect Day

12-18 Months Before the Wedding:

Create Your Budget

Determine the overall budget for your wedding

Allocate funds to different aspects like venue, catering, attire, and entertainment

Draft Your Guest List

Begin compiling a list of potential guests

Consider the size of your wedding and venue capacity

Select the Venue

Research and visit potential venues

Secure your desired date and book the venue

9-12 Months Before the Wedding:

Choose Key Suppliers

Research and select your photographer, videographer, and caterer

Book these suppliers as early as possible

Find Your Dream Attire

Start shopping for your wedding dress or suit

Allow time for fittings and alterations

Send Save-the-Dates

Inform your guests about the wedding date and location

This is particularly important for a destination wedding

6-9 Months Before the Wedding:

Finalize Guest List

Confirm the guest list and gather addresses for invitations

Consider any additional guests

Book Entertainment

Secure your preferred entertainment options, such as a DJ or live band

Choose Bridal Party Attire

Select and order dresses and suits for your bridal party

4-6 Months Before the Wedding:

Order Invitations

Design and order your wedding invitations

Include RSVP details and any additional information

Plan the Honeymoon

Research and book your honeymoon

Ensure passports and travel plans are in order

Arrange Transportation

Book transportation for the wedding day

Ensure everyone has a reliable means of reaching the venue

2-4 Months Before the Wedding:

Finalize Details

Confirm all details with suppliers

Discuss final plans with your venue coordinator

Purchase Wedding Rings

Select and purchase wedding bands for both partners

Plan Seating Arrangements

Create a seating plan for the reception

Ensure guests with special requirements are accommodated

1 Month Before the Wedding:

Final Dress Fitting

Attend your final dress or suit fitting

Confirm all alterations are completed

Finalize Payments

Confirm payment details with suppliers

Prepare vendor tips if applicable

Reconfirm Details

Reconfirm all details with suppliers, including arrival times

1-2 Weeks Before the Wedding:

Pack for the Wedding Night and Honeymoon

Prepare a bag for the wedding night and pack for the honeymoon

Finalize Wedding Timeline

Create a detailed timeline for the wedding day

Share it with your bridal party and vendors

The Big Day:

Enjoy the Moment

Trust your planning and savor every moment

Allow yourself to be fully present on your special day

Remember, this timeline is a guide, and adjustments can be made based on your unique circumstances. The key is to plan, stay organized, and most importantly, enjoy the journey to your perfect day!

Chapter 3

B udget Bliss

DO: Smart budgeting strategies

Don't: Overspending woes

Welcome to the financial heart of your wedding planning journey – "Budget Bliss." In this chapter, we'll delve into smart budgeting strategies to ensure you not only stay within your financial boundaries but also sidestep the common pitfalls of overspending unnecessarily. Planning a wedding can easily lead to getting carried away, where the initial budget seems to triple before you know it. This phenomenon is not uncommon, and unfortunately, it can detract from the joy of what should be a special time.

Having a detailed checklist with all expenses outlined is crucial for staying organized and on top of your wedding budget. Organization is key to ensuring that you don't overspend or forget important expenses. By having a checklist, you can track everything from venue costs and vendor fees to smaller details like decor and attire. This helps you stay within your budget and prevents any surprises down the line. Additionally, having a checklist allows you to prioritize expenses and allocate funds accordingly, ensuring that you're making the most of your budget without overspending in certain areas. Ultimately, a well-organized checklist is essential for keeping your wedding planning process smooth and stress-free.

Do: Smart Budgeting Strategies

Prioritize Your Expenses

Identify the most crucial elements of your wedding, such as the venue, catering, and photography

Allocate a larger portion of your budget to these priorities while being more flexible with less critical aspects

Research and Compare

Gather quotes from various vendors

Compare prices and services to ensure you're getting the best value for your budget

Create a Contingency Fund

Set aside a small percentage of your budget for unexpected expenses

This buffer will help you handle surprises without jeopardizing your overall financial plan

DIY with Caution - While DIY projects can save money, be realistic about your skills and the time involved. Ensure that the DIY projects align with your overall vision and don't become a source of stress.

Negotiate Wisely - Don't be afraid to negotiate with vendors. Many are open to adjusting packages to accommodate your budget without compromising quality.

Don't: Overspending Woes

Stick to Your Priorities

Avoid the temptation to splurge on non-essential items

Stay focused on what truly matters to you as a couple

Beware of Hidden Costs

Thoroughly review contracts to identify any hidden fees

Be transparent with vendors about your budget constraints from the beginning and regularly reassess your budget

Wedding plans can evolve, and so can your budget. Regularly reassess your financial plan and make adjustments if necessary.

Avoid Last-Minute Splurges - The excitement of nearing the wedding day can lead to impulsive spending. Resist the urge to make last-minute purchases that weren't part of your original plan.

Separate Wants from Needs- Clearly distinguish between what you want and what you need for your wedding. Allocate resources accordingly, focusing on fulfilling the essentials first.

By adopting these smart budgeting strategies and steering clear of overspending woes, you'll not only maintain financial harmony but also ensure that every dollar spent contributes to the magic of your wedding day. "Budget Bliss" is not just about limitations; it's about making conscious choices that allow you to celebrate your love without unnecessary financial stress. So, let's navigate this budgetary journey together, creating a wedding day that is both memorable and financially sound.

Learn how to allocate your budget wisely by identifying areas where splurging is worthwhile and where you can cut costs without sacrificing quality.

Another crucial aspect to consider when planning a wedding is knowing where to spend more and where to cut corners can make a significant difference in your budget without compromising on the overall experience. Here's some advice on how to allocate your funds wisely:

Splurge on What Matters Most: Identify the elements of your wedding that are most important to you and your partner, whether it's the venue, photography, or entertainment. Allocate a larger portion of your budget to these key areas to ensure you get the quality and experience you desire.

Invest in Quality Photography: Your wedding photos will be cherished memories for years to come, so it's worth investing in a talented photographer who can capture the essence of your special day. While photography packages can be expensive, quality images are priceless.

Prioritize Personalized Touches: Consider splurging on personalized details that reflect your unique style and personality, such as custom décor, specialty cocktails, or personalized favors. These special touches can elevate your wedding and make it truly memorable for you and your guests.

Focus on Guest Experience: While it's important to stay within budget, don't skimp on guest comfort and enjoyment. Allocate funds for amenities such as comfortable seating, delicious food and drinks, and entertainment to ensure your guests have a great time and feel appreciated.

Cut Corners on Non-Essentials: Look for areas where you can save money without sacrificing the overall experience. For example, consider DIY projects for décor or favors, opt for a less expensive wedding dress or groom's attire, or choose a less extravagant venue to save on rental fees.

Be Strategic with Timing: Consider hosting your wedding during the off-peak season or on a weekday to take advantage of lower prices for venues and vendors. Additionally, booking early or negotiating with vendors may result in discounts or special offers.

Stay Flexible with Your Vision: Be open to alternative options and creative solutions that can help you achieve your wedding vision within your budget. For example, consider non-traditional venues, buffet-style dining, or digital invitations to save on costs without sacrificing style.

Ultimately, the key to successful wedding planning is finding the right balance between splurging on the things that matter most to you and being strategic with your spending in other areas. You can create a beautiful and memorable wedding day that reflects your love and personality by prioritizing your budget according to your values and priorities.

Chapter 4

Crafting The Perfect Celebration

WHAT DOES THE CEREMONY symbolize? Why is selecting the ideal venue crucial for your ceremony?Ah, the ceremony, the pivotal moment you officially become a team for life, promising to weather every storm and celebrate every triumph together. It signifies the beginning of a shared journey, a union founded on love, respect, and mutual devotion. It's the part where hearts flutter, tears flow (happy tears, of course!), and love fills the air like confetti. Therefore, choosing the perfect location for this sacred event holds immense significance. But let's not forget about the other half of the equation: the reception!

Think of the reception as the ultimate celebration bash, where the real party kicks off! It's time to toss aside those fancy airs and let loose with your nearest and dearest. Imagine laughter echoing off the walls, feet tapping to the beat of the music, and glasses clinking in joyful toasts. This is your chance to indulge in delicious food, sip on signature cocktails, and dance like nobody's watching (even though everyone is, and they're loving every moment of it!). From the romantic first dance to the epic bouquet toss, every moment is a memory in the making.

And let's not forget about the cake! Whether you're into classic tiers or trendy naked cakes, this sweet confection is the cherry on top of your perfect day. So grab a slice (or two, no judgment here!) and savor every bite. But hey, the fun doesn't stop there! With photo booths, lawn games, and maybe even a surprise performance or two, there's never a dull moment at a wedding reception. It's a chance to let your hair down, kick off your shoes (literally, if you're feeling daring), and celebrate the love that brought you all together.

The venue where the all-important ceremony takes place, sets the stage for the entire experience, shaping the ambiance, atmosphere, and overall feel of the ceremony. It serves as the backdrop against which memories are made, emotions are shared, and vows are exchanged. Whether it's a majestic cathedral, a tranquil garden, or a quaint chapel, the location of the ceremony plays a vital role in capturing the essence of the couple's love story and setting the tone for the celebration that follows. Moreover, the choice of venue reflects the couple's personalities, values, and vision for their special day. It's an opportunity to express their unique style and preferences, whether they opt for a traditional setting steeped in history or a contemporary space that speaks to their modern sensibilities.

Ultimately, selecting the perfect location for the ceremony is about creating a meaningful and unforgettable experience for both the couple and their guests. It's about finding a place that resonates with the couple's hearts and souls, where they can exchange vows surrounded by beauty, love, and the warmth of those who matter most to them.

Embarking on the search for the ideal venue is a pivotal moment in your wedding planning journey as you transform your dream location into an enchanting backdrop for your celebration of love. Let's explore the dos and don'ts of choosing the perfect location for your special day and how to steer clear of common pitfalls.

Do: Choosing the Perfect Location

Define Your Vision

Clearly articulate the ambiance and style you envision for your wedding

Ensure the chosen venue aligns with your vision, whether it's a traditional church, rustic barn, a beachfront resort, or an urban loft

Consider Logistics - Evaluate the location's accessibility for both you and your guests. Check for nearby accommodations and transportation options to make the logistics seamless

Understand Venue Costs - Ask for a detailed breakdown of costs, including any hidden fees

Understand what is included in the venue package to avoid unexpected expenses

Visit Potential Venues - Schedule visits to shortlisted venues to experience the space firsthand. Take note of the atmosphere, available facilities, and any potential challenges

Check Vendor Restrictions - Inquire about any restrictions on external vendors

Ensure the venue allows the flexibility to bring in your preferred caterer, florist, and other key suppliers.

Don't: Common Venue Selection Mistakes

Ignoring Capacity Limits

Be mindful of the venue's capacity limits to avoid overcrowding, and ensure it comfortably accommodates your guest list

Overlooking the Season - Consider the season in which you plan to wed. Ensure the venue is suitable for the weather conditions during your chosen month

Falling for Aesthetics Alone - While aesthetics are crucial, don't choose a venue based solely on its appearance. Consider practical aspects such as parking, restrooms, and layout

Neglecting Guest Experience -Prioritize guest comfort and experience when selecting a venue. Consider factors like seating arrangements, flow of events, and overall guest enjoyment

Booking Without a Contract - Never book a venue without a comprehensive contract

Ensure all terms, conditions, and services are explicitly outlined to avoid misunderstandings later.

Here's a comprehensive list of options for places to get married, along with dos and don'ts, pitfalls, and best practices for each:

Religious Venue: Church, Synagogue, Mosque

Do: Respect and adhere to the religious customs and traditions of the venue.

Coordinate with clergy or officiants regarding ceremony details and requirements.

Attend pre-marital counseling or classes if required by the religious institution.

Don't: Assume all guests share the same religious beliefs or practices.

Disregard any guidelines or rules set forth by the religious institution.

Pitfalls: Limited availability for ceremonies due to regular services and events.

Restrictions on music, attire, and decor.

Best Practices: Communicate openly with clergy or officiants to ensure a meaningful and respectful ceremony. Consider incorporating personal touches or elements into the ceremony while honoring religious traditions.

Traditional Venue: Hotel, Banquet Hall, Country Club

Do: Research multiple venues to find the one that aligns with your vision and budget.

Visit potential venues in person to assess the space, ambiance, and amenities.

Negotiate pricing and contracts to ensure transparency and fairness.

Don't: Forget to inquire about hidden fees or restrictions in the venue's policies.

Assume that all-inclusive packages are the best option; sometimes, they may include services you don't need.

Pitfalls: Limited availability, especially during peak wedding seasons.

Restrictions on catering, decor, and entertainment.

Best Practices: Book well in advance to secure your desired date.

Read contracts thoroughly and clarify any uncertainties before signing.

Outdoor Venue: Garden, Beach, Vineyard

Do: Have a backup plan in case of inclement weather.

Consider the natural beauty of the surroundings as part of your decor.

Communicate with your guests about the terrain and weather conditions.

Don't: Overlook permits or permissions required for outdoor ceremonies.

Ignore the need for restroom facilities and accessibility for guests.

Pitfalls: Unpredictable weather conditions can disrupt plans.

Limited amenities compared to traditional venues.

Best Practices: Rent tents or umbrellas for shade and shelter.

Provide blankets or fans depending on the weather forecast.

Destination Wedding: Foreign Country, Tropical Island, Historic City:

Do: Research local marriage requirements and legalities.

Provide guests with ample notice and information about travel arrangements.

Work with a local wedding planner or coordinator for logistical support.

Don't: Assume all guests can afford or are willing to travel.

Neglect to factor in currency exchange rates and potential language barriers.

Pitfalls: Increased costs for travel, accommodation, and logistics.

Difficulty coordinating with vendors and suppliers from a distance.

Best Practices: Plan a pre-wedding event or excursion to spend quality time with guests.

Offer assistance and guidance for travel arrangements, such as group discounts on flights or accommodations.

Unique Venue Museum, Zoo, Library, Art Gallery

Do: Embrace the venue's ambiance and incorporate it into your theme.

Respect any rules or regulations regarding decor and setup.

Highlight the significance of the venue in your love story.

Don't: Assume all guests will be comfortable in unconventional spaces.

Overlook logistical challenges such as parking or accessibility.

Pitfalls: Limited availability for weddings due to venue schedules or regulations.

Restrictions on the use of certain areas or exhibits.

Best Practices: Work closely with venue staff to ensure a seamless event.

Consider hiring a wedding planner experienced in non-traditional venues.

At-Home Wedding: Backyard, Family Estate, Farm

Do: Capitalize on the intimate and personal atmosphere of a familiar space.

Arrange for adequate parking, restroom facilities, and accommodations if necessary.

Create a detailed layout and plan for logistics such as catering and rentals.

Don't: Underestimate the amount of time and effort required for setup and cleanup.

Overcrowd the space with unnecessary decor or furniture.

Pitfalls: Weather-dependent, which can be unpredictable for outdoor ceremonies.

Potential damage or wear to the property.

Best Practices: Rent a tent or canopy for outdoor ceremonies.

Hire professional vendors who are experienced in working in private residences.

Remember, the perfect wedding venue is not just about aesthetics or convenience; it's about finding a space that reflects your personality, values, and vision for your special day. Consider your budget, guest list, and logistical considerations when choosing the ideal location for saying "I do."

Personalizing your wedding ceremony is a wonderful way to infuse it with meaning, reflect your unique relationship, and create a memorable experience for you and your guests. Here's how you can expand on personalizing your ceremony:

Write Your Vows: Consider writing personalized vows that express your feelings, promises, and aspirations for your marriage. Share anecdotes, inside jokes, and heartfelt sentiments that reflect your relationship and journey together. This personal touch adds authenticity and emotional depth to your vows, making them even more meaningful when exchanged during the ceremony.

Incorporate Cultural or Religious Traditions: If you and your partner come from different cultural or religious backgrounds, or if you have shared traditions that hold significance to you, consider incorporating them into your ceremony. This could involve rituals, prayers, blessings, or symbolic gestures that honor your heritage and values. It's an opportunity to celebrate your diversity and create a ceremony that feels authentic to your identity.

Include Loved Ones: Involve family members, friends, or even pets in your ceremony to create a sense of community and connection. This could include asking loved ones to read poems or passages, perform musical selections, or participate in rituals such as a unity candle lighting or sand ceremony. Their participation not only adds a personal touch but also reinforces the importance of their support and presence in your lives.

Choose Meaningful Readings or Music: Select readings, poems, or song lyrics that resonate with you as a couple and convey the sentiments you wish to express on your wedding day. Whether it's a favorite love poem, a meaningful passage from a book, or a song that holds special memories, incorporating these elements into your ceremony adds layers of significance and emotion.

Design a Unique Ceremony Structure: Break away from traditional ceremony formats and design a structure that reflects your personality and values. Whether you opt for a non-linear narrative, interactive elements, or surprises, think outside the box to create a ceremony that feels authentic and reflective of your relationship dynamic.

Create Customized Rituals: Invent your own rituals or adapt existing ones to suit your preferences and beliefs. This could involve planting a tree together as a symbol of growth and longevity, exchanging meaningful gifts or keepsakes, or crafting a ceremony that incorporates elements from nature or your shared interests. Get creative and make it truly your own!

Work with an Officiant who Understands You: Choose an officiant who takes the time to get to know you as a couple and can tailor the ceremony to reflect your personality, values, and relationship. Whether it's a close friend, family member, or professional officiant, find someone who resonates with your vision and can help bring your personalized ceremony to life.

By personalizing your ceremony in these ways, you'll create a heartfelt and meaningful experience that authentically represents your love story.

Your wedding day is a time for celebration, laughter, and creating lasting memories. Let's explore the dos and don'ts that will guide you in planning a reception that radiates joy and leaves a lasting impression on both you and your guests. The reception is the perfect opportunity to continue personalizing your wedding day and create a memorable experience for you and your guests. Here's how you can make your reception truly special:

By incorporating thoughtful details and avoiding common pitfalls, your reception will be a reflection of your love story—memorable, joyful, and a perfect beginning to a lifetime of happiness. Let the revelry unfold, creating cherished moments that will be etched in your hearts forever.

Do: Planning a Memorable Reception

Themes: Do: Infuse your reception with a cohesive theme.

Example: Whether it's a vintage vibe, rustic charm, or modern elegance, a consistent theme enhances the overall experience.

Interactive Entertainment:

Do: Include interactive elements that engage and entertain guests.

Example: Photo booths, games, or a dance floor with lively music can elevate the celebratory atmosphere.

Thoughtful Seating Arrangements:

Do: Strategically plan seating arrangements to encourage mingling.

Example: Consider a mix of round tables and long banquet-style seating to facilitate conversation.

Culinary Delights:

Do: Curate a menu that caters to various tastes.

Example: Offer diverse options for appetizers, main courses, and desserts to accommodate different preferences.

Signature Drinks:

Do: Create signature drinks that reflect your personality.

Example: Craft cocktails named after meaningful aspects of your relationship add a personalized touch.

Interactive Food Stations:

Do: Incorporate interactive food stations for a dynamic culinary experience.

Example: A live carving station or a build-your-own dessert bar adds excitement.

Speeches and Toasts:

Do: Plan speeches and toasts that are heartfelt and concise.

Example: Provide a timeline for speakers to ensure a smooth flow and avoid lengthy monologues.

Photography Opportunities:

Do: Create well-lit and visually appealing spaces for photographs.

Example: Incorporate decor elements like fairy lights, backdrops, or floral arrangements to enhance photo opportunities.

Don't: Reception Regrets

Overlooking Guest Comfort

Don't neglect guest comfort during the reception.

Example: Ensure there's adequate seating, climate control, and facilities for guests' needs.

Skipping a Run-Through: Don't skip a run-through of key moments with your vendors.

Example: A rehearsal helps ensure that everyone is on the same page regarding timing and coordination.

Inadequate Bar Service: Don't skimp on bar service, leading to long wait times.

Example: Sufficient staff and well-planned bar setups contribute to a smooth and enjoyable experience.

Overloading the Schedule: Don't overload the reception schedule with too many activities.

Example: Too many events can feel rushed, leaving guests overwhelmed.

Ignoring Seating Dynamics: Don't overlook the dynamics of seating arrangements.

Example: Be mindful of relationships and preferences to create a harmonious atmosphere.

Limited Food Options: Don't offer a limited menu that may not cater to various dietary needs.

Example: Accommodate guests with diverse food preferences and allergies.

Neglecting Lighting Design: Don't neglect thoughtful lighting design.

Example: Well-planned lighting enhances the ambiance, creating a visually appealing setting.

Forgetting Vendor Meals: Don't forget to arrange meals for your vendors.

Example: Ensuring your vendors are well-fed ensures they can provide their best service throughout the event.

So here's to the reception, where love is celebrated, memories are made, and the dance floor is always calling your name! Cheers to an unforgettable night of laughter, love, and happily ever afters!

We have discussed the importance of budgeting for your event to ensure that you stay within your financial means while still creating a memorable experience for you and your guests. Let's look at two scenarios and costs associated with the venues: one for a more modest affair and another for a lavish celebration, catering to both 50 and 100 guests.

Low-Key Modest Venue:

Scenario 1: 50 Guests

Venue Rental: $500

Catering (Buffet Style): $1,500

Beverages (Beer, Wine, Soft Drinks): $500

Décor and Rentals: $500

Photographer: $800

Music (Playlist or DJ): $300

Invitations and Stationery: $200

Miscellaneous (Favors, Cake, etc.): $500

Total Budget: $5,800

Scenario 2: 100 Guests

Venue Rental: $1,000

Catering (Buffet Style): $3,000

Beverages (Beer, Wine, Soft Drinks): $800

Décor and Rentals: $1,000

Photographer: $1,500

Music (Playlist or DJ): $600

Invitations and Stationery: $300

Miscellaneous (Favors, Cake, etc.): $1,000

Total Budget: $9,200

High-End Lavish Venue:

Scenario 1: 50 Guests

Venue Rental: $2,000

Catering (Plated Dinner with Options): $3,500

Beverages (Open Bar with Premium Options): $1,500

Décor and Rentals (Floral Arrangements, Upgraded Linens): $2,000

Photographer (Includes Engagement Session): $2,000

Live Band or Entertainment: $2,000

Invitations and Stationery (Custom Design): $500

Miscellaneous (Luxury Favors, Elaborate Cake, etc.): $2,000

Total Budget: $15,500

Scenario 2: 100 Guests

Venue Rental (Upscale Venue with Exclusive Use): $5,000

Catering (Multiple-Course Meal with Wine Pairing): $7,500

Beverages (Full Bar with Top-Shelf Selections): $2,000

Décor and Rentals (Elaborate Floral Installations, Premium Table Settings): $5,000

Photographer (Includes Second Shooter and Album): $3,500

Live Band or Entertainment (Celebrity DJ or Acclaimed Band): $5,000

Invitations and Stationery (Custom Couture Design): $1,000

Miscellaneous (Luxury Gifts, Gourmet Dessert Bar, etc.): $5,000

Total Budget: $34,000

Of course, these budget estimates serve as a general guideline, and actual costs may vary based on several factors, including the chosen venue, menu selections, decorations, and other personalized touches. Here are some additional considerations to keep in mind when planning your event:

Venue Selection: Venue prices can vary widely depending on location, amenities, and exclusivity. Consider factors such as rental fees, additional charges for setup and cleanup, and any required permits or insurance.

Menu Options: Catering costs will depend on the type of cuisine, service style, and the number of guests. Keep in mind dietary restrictions and preferences when selecting menu items, as special requests may incur additional charges.

Decor and Rentals: Décor expenses can range from simple centerpieces to elaborate floral arrangements and custom installations. Rental fees for tables, chairs, linens, and other décor items should also be factored into your budget.

Photography and Entertainment: Photography and entertainment are essential elements of any event, capturing memories and setting the mood. Research photographers, bands, DJs, or other entertainment options within your budget to find the best fit for your style and preferences.

Invitations and Stationery: Custom invitations and stationery can add a personal touch to your event, but costs can vary based on design complexity, printing methods, and materials used. Consider digital options or DIY alternatives to stay within budget.

Miscellaneous Expenses: Don't forget to budget for miscellaneous expenses such as favors, cake, transportation, and any unexpected costs that may arise during the planning process.

By carefully considering these factors and prioritizing the elements that are most important to you, you can create a customized budget that aligns with your vision and financial goals. Remember to leave some flexibility in your budget for unexpected expenses or last-minute adjustments, and don't hesitate to consult with vendors or a wedding planner for guidance and assistance along the way. Remember to allocate funds based on your priorities and preferences to create an event that reflects your style and vision within your financial means.

By following these practical steps and steering clear of common pitfalls, you'll not only choose the perfect venue but also lay the foundation for a seamless and memorable wedding day.

Chapter 5

Mastering Catering and Menu Planning

CATERING AND MENU PLANNING play significant roles in shaping the overall experience of your wedding day, tantalizing guests' taste buds, and creating memorable culinary moments. Catering and menu planning are not just about satisfying hunger; they're about creating an unforgettable culinary journey for you and your guests. From the first bite of appetizers to the last sip of champagne, your wedding menu sets the tone for the entire celebration. In this chapter, we'll explore the importance of catering and menu planning in shaping the overall experience of your wedding day and provide guidance on how to create a menu that reflects your tastes, preferences, and personalities as a couple.

Food brings people together, fostering connections and creating shared experiences that transcend cultural, social, and personal boundaries. In the context of a wedding, where family and friends gather to celebrate love and union, food plays a pivotal role in enhancing the sense of community and joyous camaraderie. A wedding is not just a ceremony; it's a celebration of love, a union of two souls embarking on a lifelong journey together. It's a day filled with laughter, tears of joy, and heartfelt moments shared with loved ones. At the heart of this celebration lies the wedding feast, where guests come together to savor delicious cuisine, raise a toast, and create lasting memories.

The act of breaking bread together symbolizes unity, hospitality, and abundance, mirroring the bond between the newlyweds and their cherished guests. Whether it's a casual buffet, an elegant plated dinner, or a festive array of hors d'oeuvres, the wedding meal is an opportunity to nourish both body and soul, leaving guests feeling cherished, appreciated, and connected to the couple and each other. In this way, food serves as a catalyst for meaningful interactions and shared experiences, bringing people closer together and strengthening the bonds of love and friendship that form the foundation of the wedding celebration. From the first bite to the final toast, the wedding feast is a celebration of love, life, and the joy of coming together in the spirit of unity and harmony.are central to the success of your wedding day, ensuring that your guests are not only well-fed but also delighted by the culinary experience. From budget-friendly options to lavish feasts, your wedding menu sets the stage for a memorable celebration. In this chapter, we'll delve into the importance of thoughtful catering choices and menu planning, providing insights into pricing considerations and offering examples of menus ranging from modest to extravagant.

By carefully considering these aspects of catering and menu planning, you can create a culinary experience that reflects your unique tastes, delights your guests, and adds a touch of flavor and flair to your wedding celebration.

Understanding Your Options:

Traditional vs. Unique: Decide whether you prefer traditional wedding fare or want to explore unique and creative culinary options that reflect your tastes and personalities as a couple.

Cuisine Selection: Consider your favorite cuisines, dietary preferences, and any cultural or regional influences that you'd like to incorporate into your wedding menu.

Choosing a Caterer:

Research and Tastings: Research local catering companies, read reviews, and attend tastings to sample their offerings and determine which caterer aligns best with your vision and budget.

Customization: Look for a caterer who offers customization options to tailor the menu to your preferences and accommodate any dietary restrictions or special requests.

Menu Planning:

Appetizers and Starters: Select a variety of appetizers and starters to kick off the meal and keep guests satisfied during cocktail hour. Consider options that are both visually appealing and deliciously satisfying.

Entrees and Side Dishes: Choose a balance of entrees and side dishes that cater to different tastes and dietary needs. Offer options for meat lovers, vegetarians, and vegans, as well as gluten-free and dairy-free alternatives.

Desserts and Sweet Treats: Explore dessert options beyond the traditional wedding cake, such as dessert bars, mini desserts, or interactive stations like a s'mores bar or ice cream sundae station.

Beverage Selection:

Bar Packages: Decide on the type of bar package that best suits your preferences and budget, whether it's an open bar, cash bar, or a combination of both. Consider offering signature cocktails or a selection of wines and craft beers to complement the menu.

Non-Alcoholic Options: Don't forget about guests who prefer non-alcoholic beverages. Offer a variety of refreshing options such as mocktails, infused water stations, and specialty sodas.

Presentation and Service:

Aesthetics: Pay attention to the presentation of each dish, opting for elegant plating and stylish table settings that enhance the overall dining experience.

Service Style: Consider the style of service that best suits your wedding vibe, whether it's a formal plated dinner, buffet-style service, family-style dining, or food stations that encourage mingling and interaction among guests.

Logistics and Coordination:

Logistical Details: Work closely with your caterer to finalize logistical details such as rental equipment, staffing requirements, and setup logistics to ensure a seamless flow of service on the wedding day.

Communication: Maintain open communication with your caterer throughout the planning process to address any questions, concerns, or last-minute changes that may arise.

Tasting Experience:

Enjoyment and Feedback: Take time to savor the tasting experience and provide feedback to your caterer to fine-tune the menu and ensure that every dish meets your expectations.

Guest Experience: Keep the guest experience top of mind, aiming to delight and impress your loved ones with delicious food and impeccable service that leaves a lasting impression.

Understanding Pricing Considerations:

Factors Affecting Cost: Discuss the various factors that influence catering costs, such as the number of guests, menu selections, service style, venue requirements, and geographic location.

Budget Allocation: Offer guidance on how to allocate your wedding budget effectively, considering your priorities and preferences when it comes to catering and menu planning.

Example Menus:

a. *Budget-Friendly Menu*:

Appetizers: Assorted cheese and cracker platter, vegetable crudites with dip, mini quiches

Entrees: Chicken or vegetarian pasta with marinara sauce, roasted seasonal vegetables, garlic bread

Desserts: Assorted mini cupcakes, fruit skewers, chocolate-dipped strawberries

Beverages: Soft drinks, lemonade, iced tea

b. *Mid-Range Menu*:

Appetizers: Caprese skewers, shrimp cocktail, bruschetta

Entrees: Grilled salmon with dill sauce, herb-roasted chicken, wild rice pilaf, mixed green salad

Desserts: Miniature fruit tarts, tiramisu, assorted macarons

Beverages: Beer and wine selection, signature cocktails, sparkling water

c. *Lavish Menu:*

Appetizers: Seared scallops with mango salsa, artisanal cheese board, lobster bisque shooters

Entrees: Filet mignon with red wine reduction, lobster tail with drawn butter, truffle mashed potatoes, grilled asparagus

Desserts: Chocolate fondue station with assorted dippers, raspberry champagne cake, gourmet gelato bar

Beverages: Premium wine selection, top-shelf liquor options, champagne toast

Customization and Flexibility:

Tailoring to Preferences: Encourage couples to work with their caterer to customize menus that reflect their tastes, dietary preferences, and cultural influences.

Menu Enhancements: Discuss options for enhancing the guest experience with add-ons such as late-night snacks, specialty stations (e.g., sushi bar, taco bar), or interactive food displays.

Tips for Maximizing Value:

Seasonal Ingredients: Opt for seasonal ingredients to maximize freshness and minimize costs.

Creative Presentation: Explore creative ways to present dishes that add visual appeal without breaking the budget.

Portion Control: Consider portion sizes and service styles that strike a balance between abundance and waste.

By understanding pricing considerations and exploring example menus across different budget ranges, couples can make informed decisions that align with their financial resources while still creating a memorable and delicious culinary experience for their wedding guests.

Chapter 6

Dress Decisions

DO: FINDING THE DREAM Dress

Don't: Common Dress Shopping Mistakes

"Dress Decisions" is your passport to bridal elegance, offering insights, tips, and advice to make the process seamless and joyful. Explore reputable bridal stores in your state, and let the journey to finding your dream dress be a cherished chapter in your wedding tale. Your dress is not just a garment; it's a symbol of your love story and personal style. I'll guide you to finding the dream dress while avoiding common pitfalls during this magical journey.

Do: Finding the Dream Dress

Start Early - Commence your dress search well in advance to allow time for fittings and alterations. Bridal boutiques often require several months to order and customize your gown.

Know Your Budget - Establish a clear budget for your dress, considering alterations and accessories.

Communicate your budget to bridal consultants to streamline the selection process.

Research Styles - Explore bridal magazines, websites, and social media for inspiration.

Identify styles that resonate with your vision and body shape.

Schedule Appointments - Book appointments at bridal boutiques, ensuring personalized attention. Research and choose boutiques known for a diverse selection of dresses.

Consider the Venue - Factor in your wedding venue and theme when selecting the dress. A beach wedding may call for a lighter, flowy gown, while a formal ballroom affair may warrant a more structured design.

Bring Trusted Opinions - Invite a select few trusted friends or family members to accompany you. Ensure their opinions align with your style preferences and overall vision.

Embrace Your Body - Celebrate your body and choose a dress that enhances your favorite features. Bridal consultants can guide you to flattering styles based on your body shape.

Accessorize Mindfully - Coordinate accessories with your dress without overwhelming the overall look. Consider veils, headpieces, and jewelry that complement the gown.

Don't: Common Dress Shopping Mistakes

Ignoring Your Budget - Resist the allure of dresses outside your budget to avoid financial strain. Stick to your predetermined spending limit.

Shopping Too Early - Avoid shopping too far in advance, as trends and personal preferences may change.

Start dress shopping around 10-12 months before the wedding.

Bringing a Large Entourage - Limit the number of accompanying guests to avoid conflicting opinions. Too many voices can lead to confusion and stress.

Neglecting Alteration Costs - Factor alteration costs into your dress budget. Alterations are often necessary to achieve the perfect fit.

Overlooking Dress Codes - Consider the formality of your wedding when selecting the dress. Ensure it aligns with the dress code and ambiance of the event.

Ignoring Comfort - Prioritize comfort alongside style. You'll be wearing the dress for an entire day, so it should feel comfortable and allow easy movement.

Rushing the Decision - Take your time to make an informed decision. Rushed choices may lead to dress regret.

Designing and having a Dress made

Designing and having a dress made for your special occasion is an exciting journey, but it can also be a daunting task. Here are some tips to help you navigate the process and find the right dressmaker for you:

Research and Gather Inspiration: Start by collecting images of dresses you love. Look through bridal magazines, Pinterest boards, and online galleries to gather inspiration for your dream gown. Pay attention to styles, fabrics, and details that resonate with you.

Set a Budget: Before you begin the design process, it's essential to establish a budget for your dress. Be realistic about what you can afford and communicate this clearly with your dressmaker to ensure they can work within your budget.

Find a Reputable Dressmaker: Look for dressmakers who specialize in the style of dress you envision. Ask for recommendations from friends, family, or bridal forums, and read online reviews to gauge the reputation of potential dressmakers. Schedule consultations with a few different designers to discuss your vision and see if your personalities and aesthetics align.

Review Portfolios: During your consultations, ask to see portfolios of past work from each dressmaker. Pay attention to the quality of craftsmanship, attention to detail, and diversity of styles in their portfolio. This will give you an idea of their skill level and whether they can bring your vision to life.

Communication is Key: Clear communication is essential when working with a dressmaker. Be open and honest about your expectations, preferences, and any concerns you may have. Ask questions and listen to their recommendations and expertise to ensure you're on the same page throughout the design process.

Trust the Process: Once you've chosen a dressmaker, trust their expertise and creativity. Collaborate closely with them throughout the design process, providing feedback and input along the way. Keep an open mind and be willing to compromise on certain aspects of the design to achieve the best outcome.

Plan Ahead: Custom-made dresses take time to create, so be sure to start the process well in advance of your event date. Allow plenty of time for fittings, alterations, and any unexpected delays that may arise.

Crafting your dream dress with a skilled dressmaker can be an incredibly rewarding experience, ensuring that every detail is tailored to perfection. However, if you prefer the convenience and affordability of buying off the rack, fear not! There are plenty of stunning options available to suit all budgets and styles. Here are some examples:

Boutique Bridal Shops: These stores offer a curated selection of designer wedding dresses at various price points. You can find everything from timeless classics to modern trends, with the assistance of knowledgeable staff to help you find the perfect fit.

Sample Sales: Many bridal boutiques host sample sales where you can snag designer dresses at discounted prices. These dresses are typically floor samples or discontinued styles, offering excellent value for brides on a budget.

Online Retailers: Websites offer a wide range of wedding dresses in various styles, sizes, and price ranges. You can browse from the comfort of your home and take advantage of online sales and promotions.

Department Stores: Some department stores have bridal departments that offer a selection of wedding dresses, ranging from affordable options to designer labels. You might find hidden gems at department store sales or clearance events.

Vintage and Secondhand Shops: If you're a fan of vintage or eco-friendly fashion, consider shopping for a pre-loved wedding dress. Vintage shops and online platforms like Etsy and Stillwhite offer unique, one-of-a-kind dresses with a touch of history and charm.

Customizable Collections: Some bridal brands offer customizable collections where you can mix and match different tops, skirts, and embellishments to create your own unique look. This allows you to personalize your dress while staying within your budget.

The average cost of a wedding dress can vary greatly depending on factors such as the designer, fabric, embellishments, and location. However, at the time of writing this book, the average cost of a wedding dress in the United States ranges from $1,000 to $2,500. Keep in mind that this is just an average, and wedding dresses can cost significantly more or less depending on individual preferences and circumstances. In Australia, the average cost of a wedding dress is similar to that in the United States, ranging from approximately AUD 2,000 to $5,000. High-end designer dresses or couture gowns may exceed this average, while simpler or off-the-rack options may fall below it. As with any wedding expense, couples need to establish a budget and shop around to find a dress that fits both their style preferences and financial considerations.

Remember, the perfect wedding dress is the one that makes you feel confident, beautiful, and comfortable on your special day. Whether you choose to have it custom-made or opt for an off-the-rack option, trust your instincts and embrace the dress that speaks to your heart. After all, it's not just about the dress; it's about the love and joy you bring to it when you walk down the aisle.

Chapter 7

Guest List Guidance

DO: Crafting a balanced guest list

Don't: Navigating guest list challenges

"Guest List Guidance" is a pivotal chapter in your wedding planning journey, it is your compass in the intricate task of creating a guest list that reflects your values, priorities, and the joyous spirit of your celebration. By navigating the challenges you will assemble a guest list that contributes to the warm and inclusive atmosphere of your special day. See your guest list as a delicate tapestry, weaving together the people who matter most.

Let's explore the dos and don'ts of creating this integral element of your celebration and crafting your perfect guest list!

Do: Crafting a Balanced Guest List

Define Your Priorities - Clarify your priorities and values in creating the guest list. Identify must-invite guests, such as immediate family and closest friends.

Set Clear Criteria - Establish clear criteria for inviting guests, considering relationships, and the significance of their presence. Prioritize those who have played a meaningful role in your lives.

Consider Venue Capacity - Be mindful of your venue's capacity when finalizing the guest list. Ensure there's ample space for everyone to comfortably celebrate.

Communicate with Your Partner - Maintain open communication with your partner throughout the guest list creation. Collaborate on decisions to ensure a fair representation of both sides.

Create Guest List Categories - Group guests into categories to streamline decision-making. Categories might include family, close friends, extended family, and work colleagues.

Utilize A & B Lists - Consider an A and B list approach for managing limited space. Send invitations to the A list first, and if RSVPs allow, invite additional guests from the B list.

Don't: Navigating Guest List Challenges

Overcrowding for Obligation - Avoid inviting guests out of obligation rather than genuine connection. Prioritize those who have played active roles in your lives.

Ignoring Budget Constraints - Be conscious of your budget when finalizing the guest list. Remember that each additional guest incurs additional costs for catering and other elements.

Last-Minute Additions - Resist making last-minute additions to the guest list without careful consideration. Sudden changes can impact seating arrangements and catering plans.

Family Feuds and Friendships - Navigate family feuds and friendship dynamics with sensitivity. Consider the potential impact of certain guests on the overall atmosphere.

Assuming Everyone Can Attend - Avoid assuming that every guest can attend. Be prepared for some declines and plan accordingly.

Not Sending Save-the-Dates Early - Ensure you send save-the-dates well in advance. This gives guests ample time to make arrangements and avoids last-minute conflicts.

Navigating the guest list can be challenging, for some, it's the most stressful part of planning, especially when there are tensions or conflicts among certain individuals. Clear communication is the key to navigating potential conflicts and ensuring that your wedding day is a memorable and harmonious celebration.

Here's how to handle it:

Define Your Priorities: Start by outlining your priorities for the guest list. Identify must-invite guests, such as immediate family and close friends, and consider whether certain individuals should be included despite any conflicts.

Communicate with Your Partner: Have an open and honest conversation with your partner about who you both want to invite and any concerns you may have about specific guests.

Set Boundaries: While it's essential to be considerate of family dynamics, remember that it's your wedding day, and you have the right to set boundaries. If there are individuals who shouldn't be seated together, communicate your preferences to your wedding planner or venue coordinator.

Consider Separate Events: If tensions are particularly high between certain individuals, consider hosting separate events, such as a rehearsal dinner or post-wedding brunch, where they won't have to interact.

Seat Assignments: Take extra care when creating seating arrangements to ensure that guests who don't get along are seated apart. Utilize escort cards or a seating chart to strategically place guests.

Preemptive Conversations: If you anticipate conflicts, consider having preemptive conversations with the individuals involved. Express your desire for a peaceful celebration and ask for their cooperation in maintaining harmony.

Limit Alcohol: Limiting alcohol consumption during the event can help prevent tensions from escalating.

Designate Mediators: Enlist the help of trusted friends or family members to act as mediators if conflicts arise during the event.

Focus on the Positive: Remind yourself and your guests that this is a joyous occasion to celebrate your love and commitment. Encourage everyone to focus on the positive aspects of the day.

Professional Help: If tensions are particularly high or you're unsure how to handle specific situations, consider seeking advice from a wedding planner or family therapist who specializes in managing family dynamics.

The last thing you want is for guests to feel uneasy and unable to fully enjoy the event. A wedding is a remarkable occasion, symbolizing the union of two individuals in love. It's an opportunity for everyone to come together, set aside any grievances, and revel in the joyous celebration of love and commitment.

Chapter 8

I nvitation Etiquette

DO: Designing and sending perfect invitations

Don't: Invitation faux pas to avoid

"Invitation Etiquette" marks a significant milestone in your wedding planning, as it sets the tone for your guests and provides them with a glimpse of the celebration to come. Crafting and sending invitations require finesse and attention to detail. Let's explore the dos and don'ts to ensure your invitations are a harmonious prelude to your special day.

Do: Designing and Sending Perfect Invitations

Start Early - Begin the invitation process well in advance to allow time for design, printing, and addressing. Aim to send invitations 8-12 weeks before the wedding date.

Reflect Your Theme - Design invitations that reflect the theme and colors of your wedding. Consistent aesthetics create a cohesive and memorable experience.

State Details - Include all essential information – date, time, venue, and RSVP details.

Clearly state whether the invitation is for the ceremony and reception or just the reception.

Personalize Invitations - Add personal touches that reflect your personality. Consider handwritten elements or custom illustrations for a unique touch.

Consider RSVP Options - Provide convenient RSVP options, whether through a pre-stamped card, online form, or wedding website. Set a reasonable RSVP deadline to allow for finalizing details.

Proofread Carefully -Thoroughly proofread the invitation for any errors. Have a second set of eyes review the text to catch any overlooked mistakes.

Include Accommodation Information - If many guests are traveling, include information on local accommodations. Provide hotel options and any booking codes for special rates.

Use Proper Wording - Choose wording that suits the formality of your wedding.

Traditional or contemporary wording can set the tone for the event.

Don't: Invitation Faux Pas to Avoid

Overlooking Postage - Ensure you have the correct postage for your invitations. Square or bulky invitations may require additional postage.

Including Registry Details: Avoid including registry information on the invitation. Share registry details through word of mouth or on your wedding website.

Electronic Invitations for Formal Events - Formal weddings generally call for traditional paper invitations however e-invitations or digital invitations are more budget-friendly than paper and have become increasingly popular for weddings and other events due to their convenience, eco-friendliness, and cost-effectiveness allowing you to track RSVPs in real-time, send reminders, and update event details effortlessly.

Sending Invitations Too Late - Avoid sending invitations too close to the wedding date. Guests need ample time to plan and RSVP.

Overcomplicating Design - Keep the design clean and straightforward. Overly intricate designs may distract from essential information.

Ignoring RSVP Deadline - Stick to your RSVP deadline for accurate guest count. Late RSVPs can complicate seating arrangements and catering plans.

Forgetting Plus-Ones - Clearly state whether a guest is invited with a plus-one.

Avoid assumptions or vague wording that may lead to confusion. Certainly, addressing wedding invitations can be delicate, especially when considering various family dynamics. Here are examples of how to address invitations in different situations:

Deceased Parent - If one or both parents are deceased, you can include a respectful mention using wording such as: "Together with their families, [Your Full Name] & [Partner's Full Name] invite you to celebrate their wedding."

Divorced Parents Hosting Together - When divorced parents are hosting together, consider: "Mr. [Father's Full Name] and Mrs. [Mother's Full Name] request the pleasure of your company at the wedding of their daughter, [Your Full Name] to [Partner's Full Name]."

Divorced Parents Hosting Separately - In the case of divorced parents hosting separate events, you may use: "Mr. [Father's Full Name] requests the pleasure of your company at the wedding of his daughter, [Your Full Name] to [Partner's Full Name]. [Location and Date]" or "Mrs. [Mother's Full Name] requests the pleasure of your company at the wedding reception of her daughter, [Your Full Name] and [Partner's Full Name]. [Location and Date]"

No Parents Hosting (Couple Hosting) - When the couple is hosting the wedding themselves, you can use: "Together with joyous hearts, [Your Full Name] and [Partner's Full Name] invite you to celebrate their wedding."

Remember, the key is to be respectful and considerate of everyone involved. If you're uncertain about how to address the invitations, it's always a good idea to communicate openly with family members and, if needed, seek their input on the wording.

Chapter 9

The Heart of Your Wedding - Why Your Vows Matter

PICTURE THIS: YOU'RE standing hand in hand, gazing into the eyes of your beloved, surrounded by friends and family. The music swells, the atmosphere crackles with anticipation, and then... it's time for the vows. In that moment, it's not just a formality; it's the beating heart of your wedding day. Let's talk about why those vows you're about to exchange matter. We're not just talking about the words you recite; we're talking about the promises you make that will shape the rest of your lives together.

In this chapter, we're diving deep into the world of personalized vows. We'll explore why they're so much more than just a tradition, and how crafting them can be a journey of self-discovery and love. Crafting personalized wedding vows is a journey that goes far beyond the surface level of tradition. It's an intimate exploration of the unique bond shared between two individuals, a heartfelt expression of their deepest emotions, values, and promises to one another.

When couples embark on the journey of writing their own vows, they are essentially delving into the depths of their relationship, uncovering the essence of what makes their love story special and enduring. It's a process of reflection, introspection, and soul-searching as they sift through memories, experiences, and shared moments that have shaped their journey together.

Through the act of crafting vows, couples have the opportunity to articulate their feelings in a way that is authentic and deeply personal. They can express their love, gratitude, and admiration for each other, acknowledging the strengths and challenges that have strengthened their bond over time. Moreover, writing vows can be a transformative experience, allowing couples to confront their fears, insecurities, and vulnerabilities with courage and honesty. It's a moment of profound vulnerability as they stand before each other and declare their deepest desires, hopes, and intentions for the future.

In this journey of self-discovery, couples may uncover newfound depths of understanding and appreciation for each other. They may realize the power of their love to overcome obstacles, to inspire growth, and to bring out the best in one another. But perhaps most importantly, crafting personalized vows is an act of love in itself. It's a declaration of commitment and devotion, a promise to stand by each other through thick and thin, to support each other's dreams and aspirations, and to cherish the bond they share for a lifetime.

As couples exchange their vows on their wedding day, they are not just reciting words; they are affirming the sacred covenant they are entering into—a covenant rooted in love, respect, and mutual understanding. And as they embark on this new chapter of their lives together, they carry with them the profound significance of their vows, serving as guiding beacons of light, love, and hope for the journey ahead.

Here are some sample heartfelt vows:

Example 1:

My beloved [Partner's Name],

Today, as we stand before our loved ones, I vow to cherish and honor you for all the days of my life. From this moment forward, I promise to be your steadfast companion, your confidant, and your biggest supporter. I vow to listen to you with an open heart and to speak to you with honesty and kindness.

I promise to stand by your side through every triumph and challenge, to celebrate your joys and share in your sorrows. I promise to respect your individuality and to support your dreams, knowing that together, we are stronger than we could ever be apart.

I pledge to love you unconditionally, to laugh with you in times of joy, and to comfort you in times of sorrow. I promise to be patient and understanding, to forgive you your faults as I hope you will forgive mine.

Above all, I vow to be true to you, to cherish you, and to love you with all my heart, for all the days of my life.

Example 2:

"[Partner's Name], from the moment we met, I knew that you were the one I wanted to spend my life with. Today, as I stand before you, I pledge my love, my loyalty, and my unwavering support to you.

I promise to cherish every moment we share together, to laugh with you in times of joy, and to comfort you in times of sorrow. I promise to be your partner in adventure, your confidant in times of uncertainty, and your rock when you need strength.

I vow to respect you as an individual, to honor your dreams and aspirations, and to encourage you to pursue your passions. I promise to listen with an open heart, to communicate honestly and openly, and to always strive to understand and empathize with your perspective.

I promise to be your faithful companion, your equal partner, and your greatest advocate in life. With all that I am and all that I have, I take you as my beloved [Partner's Name], to love and to cherish, from this day forward, until the end of time.

Example 3:

As I stand here today, surrounded by our loved ones, I am filled with an overwhelming sense of gratitude for the love we share. You are my best friend, my soulmate, and my greatest blessing.

I promise to be your unwavering supporter, your biggest cheerleader, and your shoulder to lean on in times of need. I promise to celebrate your successes, to lift you up when you falter, and to stand by your side through every triumph and challenge that life brings our way.

I vow to honor and respect you as an individual, to cherish the unique qualities that make you who you are, and to nurture the beautiful soul that you possess.

I promise to be patient, and kind, and to always choose love in every situation we encounter.

I pledge to create a life filled with laughter, adventure, and endless possibilities with you. Together, we will build a home filled with love, understanding, and acceptance. With my whole heart, I take you as my partner, my love, and my companion, now and forevermore.

Example 4:

As we stand here today, surrounded by our loved ones, I am reminded of all the moments, big and small, that have brought us to this point.

From the laughter-filled adventures to the quiet moments of shared silence, each experience has shaped us and strengthened our bond. And so, as we exchange our vows, I pledge to honor and cherish every aspect of our unique relationship. I promise to embrace your quirks and idiosyncrasies, knowing that they are what make you who you are—the person I fell in love with. I vow to be your partner in every sense of the word, walking beside you through life's highs and lows, holding your hand through every twist and turn.

Together, we have weathered storms and basked in the warmth of sunshine. And as we embark on this new chapter together, I promise to be your anchor in the storm, your shelter in the rain, and your beacon of light in the darkness.

I promise to support your dreams, to celebrate your victories, and to lift you when you stumble. I vow to be your confidant, your ally, and your safe harbor, offering you the unwavering love and acceptance that you deserve.

With every beat of my heart, I take you as my partner, my love, and my best friend. And with these vows, I pledge to love you unconditionally, to honor you wholeheartedly, and to cherish our unique bond for all the days of my life.

When it comes to personalized vows, it's important to remember that there is no right or wrong way to express your love and commitment. It's about infusing the essence of your unique relationship and experiences together, a beautiful journey of exploration and discovery. Your vows should reflect your unique relationship, values, and promises to each other. Whether you choose to recite traditional vows, write your own from scratch, or incorporate elements of both, the most important thing is that your vows come from the heart and resonate with you and your partner. So, embrace your individuality, speak from the heart, and cherish the moment as you share your love. It's a chance to delve deep into the essence of your relationship and express the love, commitment, and promises that bind you together.

Chapter 10

Crafting Your Dream Wedding

WEDDING CAKE AND DESSERTS:

Planning Process: Discuss the process of selecting and designing your wedding cake and desserts. This may involve researching bakeries or pastry chefs, scheduling tastings, and collaborating on flavor and design options.

Budget Considerations: Guide budgeting for your wedding cake and desserts, including factors such as size, complexity of design, and additional dessert options (e.g., cupcakes, macarons, dessert bars).

Dietary Restrictions: Discuss how to accommodate guests with dietary restrictions or preferences, such as offering gluten-free, dairy-free, or vegan options.

Presentation and Display: Explore creative ideas for presenting and displaying your wedding cake and desserts, such as custom cake stands, dessert tables, or themed displays that complement your wedding decor.

Bridal Beauty Preparation:

Hair Styling: Professional hairstylists can create a variety of hairstyles to complement your wedding dress, theme, and personal style. From elegant updos and romantic curls to sleek blowouts and bohemian braids, they can bring your vision to life.

Makeup Application: Makeup artists specialize in creating flawless makeup looks that enhance your natural features and withstand the demands of the wedding day. They can achieve a range of looks, from natural and dewy to glamorous and bold, ensuring that you feel confident and radiant.

Personalized Consultation:

Trial Run: Before the wedding day, many hair and makeup artists offer trial sessions where you can test different styles and looks to find the perfect combination for your wedding. This allows you to communicate your preferences and make any adjustments before the big day.

Customization: Hair and makeup artists tailor their services to suit your individual preferences, taking into account factors such as your facial features, skin tone, dress style, and overall wedding aesthetic. They collaborate with you to create a look that reflects your personality and vision.

Efficiency and Convenience:

On-Site Services: Many hair and makeup artists offer on-site services, meaning they come to your location on the wedding day to provide hair and makeup services for you and your bridal party. This saves time and eliminates the need for travel, allowing you to relax and enjoy the morning with your loved ones.

Timely Execution: Professional hair and makeup artists are skilled at managing their time effectively to ensure that everyone is ready on schedule. They work efficiently while maintaining a relaxed and enjoyable atmosphere, helping to alleviate stress and nerves on the wedding day.

Long-Lasting Results:

Quality Products and Techniques: Experienced hair and makeup artists use high-quality products and techniques that are designed to withstand the rigors of the wedding day, including tears, hugs, and dancing. They ensure that your hair and makeup look fresh and flawless from the ceremony to the reception.

Touch-Up Services: Some hair and makeup artists offer touch-up services throughout the day to ensure that you look your best in photos and maintain your confidence on the dance floor. This extra level of service provides peace of mind and allows you to focus on enjoying the celebration.

Overall, hair and makeup services on the wedding day are an integral part of crafting your wedding vision, helping you look and feel beautiful as you walk down the aisle and celebrate this momentous occasion with your loved ones.

Photography and Videography:

Vendor Selection: Offer tips for selecting the right photographer and videographer for your wedding day. This may involve researching portfolios, reading reviews, and scheduling consultations to discuss your vision and expectations.

Coverage and Packages: Discuss different photography and videography packages available, including options for engagement sessions, full-day coverage, additional shooters, and post-production services (e.g., editing, and album design).

Shot List and Timeline: Emphasize the importance of creating a shot list and timeline with your photographer and videographer to ensure that all important moments are captured on your wedding day.

Communication and Collaboration: Encourage open communication and collaboration with your photographer and videographer throughout the planning process, from discussing shot preferences to coordinating logistics on the wedding day.

Floral Design and Decor:

Floral Consultation: Guide couples through the process of working with a florist to design their wedding florals. This may involve scheduling a consultation and discussing color palettes, flower choices, and overall design aesthetics.

Budgeting for Florals: Provide guidance on budgeting for wedding florals, including considerations such as types of arrangements (bouquets, centerpieces, ceremony decor), seasonal availability, and any additional decor elements (e.g., arches, garlands, floral installations).

Sustainability and Seasonality: Discuss the importance of considering sustainability and seasonality when choosing wedding florals, including options for locally sourced, eco-friendly flowers and greenery.

Decor and Styling: Explore creative ways to incorporate florals into your wedding decor and styling, from aisle markers and table centerpieces to floral backdrops and statement installations.

Music and Entertainment:

Entertainment Options: Discuss different entertainment options for your wedding day, including live bands, DJs, solo musicians, and other performers. Consider factors such as musical preferences, venue size, and budget when making your selection.

Creating a Playlist: Provide tips for creating a wedding playlist that reflects your musical tastes and sets the mood for each part of your wedding day, from the ceremony and cocktail hour to the reception and dancing.

Special Performances: Explore the possibility of incorporating special performances or entertainment acts into your wedding day, such as dancers, acrobats, or cultural performers, to surprise and delight your guests.

Interactive Elements: Discuss ideas for interactive entertainment elements that engage guests and create memorable experiences, such as photo booths, lawn games, or themed activities that tie into your wedding theme or interests.

Transportation and Accommodations:

Guest Accommodations: Guide on securing accommodations for out-of-town guests, including booking room blocks at nearby hotels and providing information on local attractions and amenities.

Transportation Logistics: Discuss options for transportation on your wedding day, including arranging shuttle services for guests between the ceremony and reception venues, hiring limousines or vintage cars for the bridal party, and coordinating transportation for guests with special needs.

Parking and Directions: Offer tips for providing clear directions and parking instructions for guests attending your wedding, including maps, signage, and digital resources to help guests navigate to and from the venue.

Accessibility Considerations: Emphasize the importance of considering accessibility needs when planning transportation and accommodations for guests, including wheelchair accessibility, accessible parking, and accommodations for guests with mobility issues or disabilities.

Wedding Party Roles and Responsibilities:

Bridal Party Duties: Outline the roles and responsibilities of the bridal party, including bridesmaids, groomsmen, maid of honor, best man, and other members of the wedding party. This may include assisting with wedding planning tasks, attending pre-wedding events, and providing emotional support to the couple.

Communication and Coordination: Discuss the importance of clear communication and coordination between the couple and their wedding party, including regular updates on wedding plans, timelines, and expectations for the wedding day.

Support and Encouragement: Encourage couples to express gratitude and appreciation for their wedding party's support and contributions throughout the planning process, from attending dress fittings and rehearsals to helping with DIY projects and day-of logistics.

Personalized Thank-You Gifts: Provide ideas for personalized thank-you gifts for members of the wedding party, such as monogrammed items, custom jewelry, or experiential gifts that reflect their interests and personalities.

By exploring these topics in-depth, you may both gain a better understanding of the planning process and make informed decisions that reflect your unique vision and priorities for your wedding day.

Chapter 11

Smooth Sailing on the Day

"SMOOTH SAILING ON THE Day" is the culmination of your wedding planning efforts. It is your guide to navigating the wedding day with grace and composure. By creating a well-thought-out timeline and anticipating common hiccups, you'll set the stage for a joyous and unforgettable celebration. As the day approaches, meticulous preparation becomes your anchor for a stress-free celebration. In this chapter, we'll explore the dos and don'ts that will guide you through the wedding day with ease and joy. Let the final chapter of your wedding planning journey be a testament to your meticulous preparation and the beginning of a beautiful union.

When the wedding day finally arrives, ensuring that it runs smoothly and stress-free becomes paramount for both the couple and their guests. The wedding day is a culmination of months, or even years, of planning, anticipation, and excitement. For the couple, it's a deeply emotional and significant milestone in their relationship. A smoothly executed day allows them to fully immerse themselves in the moment, savoring every precious second without the distraction of logistical hiccups or unexpected challenges.

The happiness and comfort of the guests are also of utmost importance. They have likely traveled from near and far to celebrate the couple's special day, and their experience should be seamless and enjoyable. From the ceremony to the reception, guests should feel welcomed, well-cared-for, and able to focus on sharing in the joy of the occasion. A smoothly run wedding day ensures that all planned events and activities unfold as envisioned, maximizing opportunities for creating lasting memories. Whether it's the first look between the couple, heartfelt speeches from loved ones, or spontaneous moments on the dance floor, each element contributes to the overall magic of the day.

A well-executed wedding day relies on effective coordination among various vendors, including caterers, florists, photographers, and musicians. When everyone is on the same page and working together seamlessly, it minimizes the risk of delays, misunderstandings, or errors that could disrupt the flow of the day. Planning a wedding can be incredibly stressful, and the last thing any couple wants is to feel overwhelmed or frazzled on their big day. A smoothly run wedding day allows the couple to relax, enjoy, and be fully present at the moment, free from worries about logistics or mishaps.

The wedding day often flies by in a blur of excitement and emotion. Professional photographers and videographers are tasked with capturing every precious moment, from the bride's walk down the aisle to the grand exit at the end of the night. A smoothly run day ensures that these professionals have ample opportunities to document the day's highlights without interruptions or disruptions. Ultimately, a smoothly run wedding day contributes to the overall satisfaction of everyone involved, from the couple and their families to the guests and vendors. It leaves a positive impression and reinforces the feeling that all the time, effort, and resources invested in planning the wedding were well worth it.

In conclusion, the importance of ensuring that the wedding day runs smoothly and stress-free cannot be overstated. It sets the stage for a memorable and joyous celebration, allowing the couple and their loved ones to cherish every moment and create cherished memories that will last a lifetime.

Here is a checklist for smooth sailing on the day:

Do: Creating a Day-of Timeline

Early Morning Preparations:

Do: Begin the day with ample time for hair, makeup, and pre-ceremony rituals.

Example: Schedule beauty appointments well in advance to avoid the rush and ensure a relaxed morning.

Photography Sessions:

Do: Plan photography sessions strategically, allowing time for portraits, group shots, and candid moments.

Example: Allocate specific time slots for each photography session, considering the lighting conditions.

Ceremony Timing:

Do: Set a realistic timeline for the ceremony, including the processional, vows, and recessional.

Example: Ensure there's a buffer before the ceremony for any unexpected delays.

Transition to Reception:

Do: Smoothly transition from the ceremony to the reception, factoring in travel time.

Example: Arrange transportation for the wedding party to avoid delays in reaching the reception venue.

Reception Highlights:

Do: Plan key moments during the reception, such as the first dance, toasts, and cake cutting.

Example: Create a detailed timeline for the reception, ensuring a seamless flow of events.

Vendor Coordination:

Do: Communicate with vendors about the timeline and any specific requirements.

Example: Share the timeline with the catering team, ensuring they are aware of when to serve meals and refreshments.

Guest Interaction:

Do: Allow time for mingling with guests and expressing gratitude.

Example: Plan a moment during the reception to personally thank guests for being part of your special day.

Don't: Common Wedding Day Hiccups

Overcomplicating the Schedule:

Don't: Overload the day with too many activities and tight schedules.

Example: Avoid planning back-to-back events that could lead to stress and exhaustion.

Ignoring Contingency Plans:

Don't: Overlook contingency plans for unexpected situations like weather changes.

Example: Have a backup plan for an outdoor ceremony in case of rain.

Forgetting Essentials:

Don't: Forget essential items needed during the day.

Example: Ensure someone has the wedding rings and any crucial documents.

Not Communicating Changes:

Don't: Make last-minute changes without informing key individuals.

Example: If there's a change in the schedule, communicate it promptly to the wedding party and vendors.

Neglecting Comfort:

Don't: Forget to consider the comfort of the wedding party and guests.

Example: Provide shade, seating, and refreshments, especially in outdoor settings.

Stressing Over Perfection:

Don't: Stress over minor imperfections.

Example: Understand that small details might not go as planned, but the overall experience is what matters most.

Failing to Delegate:

Don't: Try to manage everything yourself.

Example: Delegate tasks to trusted individuals, such as a wedding coordinator, to handle logistics.

While weddings are often associated with perfection, unexpected mishaps can occur, even with meticulous planning and preparation, it's essential to acknowledge that challenges may arise on the wedding day turning what was meant to be flawless into a memorable adventure.

Here are a few examples of weddings where things didn't go according to plan;

Weather Woes: Outdoor weddings are at the mercy of Mother Nature, and unexpected weather changes can throw a wrench into carefully laid plans. Imagine a beautiful beach ceremony disrupted by an unexpected rainstorm or a scorching heatwave during an outdoor summer wedding. Couples may need to quickly relocate to a backup indoor venue or provide umbrellas and fans for guests.

Transportation Troubles: Transportation issues can cause delays and stress on the wedding day. Whether it's a limo breaking down on the way to the ceremony, traffic jams causing guests to arrive late, or difficulty finding parking at the venue, logistical challenges can test the couple's patience and adaptability.

Wardrobe Malfunctions: Wardrobe mishaps can happen to even the most prepared couples. From a torn wedding dress to a missing groom's suit jacket, unexpected wardrobe malfunctions can cause panic and stress. Quick fixes such as sewing kits, safety pins, or borrowing attire from bridal party members can help salvage the situation.

Vendor No-Shows: Despite thorough planning and communication, there's always a risk of vendors failing to show up on the wedding day. Whether it's the DJ canceling last minute or the florist delivering the wrong flowers, unexpected vendor issues can throw off the entire schedule. Having backup plans and alternative contacts can help mitigate the impact of vendor no-shows.

Technical Glitches: In today's digital age, technology can be both a blessing and a curse. Imagine the horror of a microphone failing during the ceremony, a photographer's camera malfunctioning, or the DJ's sound system crashing mid-reception. Couples may need to think on their feet and find creative solutions to keep the festivities going smoothly.

Guest Drama: Family dynamics and interpersonal conflicts can sometimes spill over into the wedding day, causing tension and drama. Whether it's a heated argument between relatives or unexpected guests crashing the event, couples may need to navigate delicate situations with diplomacy and grace to ensure

Here are some tips and strategies to help you through:

Stay Calm: As the saying goes, "Keep calm and carry on." Maintaining a calm demeanor, especially as the couple, sets the tone for how others will react to the situation. Take a deep breath, remind yourself of the significance of the day, and focus on finding solutions rather than dwelling on the problem.

Delegate Responsibilities: You've likely enlisted the help of friends, family members, or wedding planners to assist with various aspects of the wedding. Delegate responsibilities to trusted individuals who can help troubleshoot issues as they arise. Having a support system in place can alleviate stress and ensure that tasks are addressed efficiently.

Problem-Solve: Approach the situation with a problem-solving mindset. Identify the root cause of the issue and brainstorm possible solutions. Consider alternative options or workarounds that can mitigate the impact of the problem while keeping the overall vision of the wedding intact.

Communicate Effectively: Clear and open communication is key when addressing unexpected challenges. Keep all stakeholders informed of the situation, including vendors, wedding party members, and guests, as appropriate. Transparency helps manage expectations and ensures that everyone is on the same page when it comes to implementing solutions.

Prioritize: Not all problems are created equal, and some may require immediate attention while others can be addressed later. Prioritize tasks based on their urgency and impact on the overall flow of the wedding day. Focus on resolving critical issues first before tackling less pressing concerns.

Maintain Perspective: While it's natural to feel disappointed or frustrated when things don't go as planned, it's essential to keep things in perspective. Remember the reason you're celebrating – your love and commitment to each other. At the end of the day, it's the marriage that truly matters, not the minor mishaps that may occur during the wedding festivities.

Adapt and Embrace: Sometimes, the best-laid plans go awry, and that's okay. Embrace the unexpected as part of your wedding day story. Adapt to the circumstances with grace and flexibility, knowing that these challenges will become cherished memories in the years to come. After all, it's often the imperfections that make the day uniquely yours.

While these examples may seem like potential disasters, they often become cherished memories in hindsight. Couples who embrace the unexpected with humor, flexibility, and resilience can turn even the most challenging situations into memorable moments that add character and depth to their wedding day story.

By maintaining composure, enlisting support, and approaching challenges with a positive attitude, you can navigate any unexpected bumps in the road and ensure that your wedding day remains a joyous and unforgettable celebration of love. Amidst the chaos and unpredictability of wedding planning and the wedding day itself, it's crucial to remember what truly matters: love, commitment, and the celebration of a lifelong partnership. No matter what unexpected challenges or mishaps may arise, keeping sight of the core values and emotions that brought you and your partner together can help put things into perspective. At the end of the day, it's the love shared between two people and the support of friends and family that make the wedding day truly special and memorable. So, take a deep breath, focus on each other, and embrace the journey together, knowing that love will always be the guiding force through it all.

Chapter 12

An Unforgettable Honeymoon Experience

THE HONEYMOON MARKS the beginning of your romantic journey as a newly married couple. This chapter delves into the dos and don'ts of planning a dream honeymoon, ensuring that your first adventure as a spouse is filled with love, relaxation, and unforgettable moments.

The honeymoon is a time for newlyweds to embark on a journey of romance, relaxation, and adventure as they celebrate their love and begin their married life together. In this chapter, we'll explore the importance of the honeymoon as a cherished tradition and offer guidance on planning and crafting the perfect romantic getaway.

Understanding the Significance of the Honeymoon:

Celebrating Newlywed Bliss: The honeymoon is a time for newlyweds to bask in the glow of their recent nuptials and enjoy some quality time together away from the hustle and bustle of everyday life.

Creating Lasting Memories: It's an opportunity to create cherished memories that will last a lifetime, from romantic dinners on the beach to thrilling adventures in exotic destinations.

Building Stronger Bonds: The honeymoon allows couples to strengthen their bond and deepen their connection as they embark on this new chapter of their lives together.

Choosing the Perfect Destination:

Considerations and Preferences: Discuss factors to consider when choosing a honeymoon destination, such as budget, travel preferences, time of year, and desired activities (e.g., beach relaxation, cultural exploration, adventure).

Dream Destinations: Explore popular honeymoon destinations around the world, from tropical paradises like the Maldives and Bali to romantic European cities like Paris and Venice, offering inspiration for couples with different interests and tastes.

Personalization: Encourage couples to personalize their honeymoon experience to reflect their unique interests and personalities, whether it's a secluded beach retreat, a luxury safari, or a cultural immersion in a vibrant city.

Planning and Logistics:

Budgeting and Financial Considerations: *Guide budgeting for the honeymoon, including* tips for saving money, maximizing travel rewards, and finding deals and discounts.

Travel Arrangements: Discuss the logistics of booking flights, accommodations, transportation, and activities, emphasizing the importance of planning ahead to secure the best options and avoid last-minute stress.

Travel Documents and Insurance: Remind couples to ensure that they have valid passports, visas, and any necessary travel documents, as well as travel insurance to protect against unforeseen circumstances.

Creating Unforgettable Experiences:

Romantic Activities: Offer suggestions for romantic activities and experiences to enjoy together on the honeymoon, such as sunset cruises, couples' massages, private dinners, and stargazing under the night sky.

Adventure and Exploration: Explore opportunities for adventure and exploration, from snorkeling in crystal-clear waters and hiking to hidden waterfalls to exploring ancient ruins and sampling local cuisine.

Balancing Relaxation and Adventure: Encourage couples to strike a balance between relaxation and adventure, allowing time for both leisurely lounging by the pool and exciting excursions and sightseeing.

Capturing Memories and Moments:

Photography and Keepsakes: Remind couples to capture special moments and memories from their honeymoon through photographs, videos, and keepsakes, creating tangible reminders of their magical getaway.

Journaling and Reflection: Encourage couples to journal about their experiences and reflections during the honeymoon, documenting their thoughts, feelings, and highlights from this special time together.

Post-Honeymoon Reflections:

Bringing Home the Magic: As the honeymoon comes to an end, encourage couples to reflect on their experiences and reminisce about the memories they've created together. Discuss ways to keep the honeymoon spirit alive in their everyday lives and continue nurturing their relationship long after the trip is over.

The honeymoon is a once-in-a-lifetime opportunity for newlyweds to celebrate their love and begin their married life with an unforgettable adventure. By planning and crafting the perfect romantic getaway, couples can create cherished memories and strengthen their bond as they embark on this new chapter together. Whether it's a tropical paradise, a European escape, or an off-the-beaten-path adventure, the honeymoon is a time to indulge in romance, relaxation, and adventure, setting the stage for a lifetime of love and happiness.

Do: Planning a Dream Honeymoon

Early Research:

Do: Begin researching and planning your honeymoon well in advance.

Example: Research destination options, accommodation, and activities to secure the best deals.

Consider Interests:

Do: Choose a destination that aligns with both your interests.

Example: If you love adventure, opt for a destination that offers thrilling activities; if relaxation is a priority, choose a tranquil retreat.

Budget Wisely:

Do: Establish a realistic budget for your honeymoon.

Example: Allocate funds for travel, accommodation, meals, and activities to ensure financial comfort.

Personalized Itinerary:

Do: Create a personalized itinerary that includes a mix of relaxation and exploration.

Example: Blend days of leisure by the beach with excursions to local attractions.

Surprise Element:

Do: Include a surprise element to make the honeymoon special.

Example: Plan a surprise romantic dinner, spa treatment, or an unexpected excursion.

Capture Moments:

Do: Bring a camera or use your smartphone to capture special moments.

Example: Documenting your honeymoon allows you to relive the memories in the years to come.

Travel Insurance:

Do: Invest in comprehensive travel insurance.

Example: Ensure coverage for unexpected events, including trip cancellations, medical emergencies, or lost belongings.

Local Cuisine Exploration:

Do: Explore and savor the local cuisine of your honeymoon destination.

Example: Trying authentic dishes adds a cultural dimension to your experience.

Don't: Honeymoon Planning Missteps

Last-Minute Planning:

Don't: Leave honeymoon planning to the last minute.

Example: Last-minute arrangements may limit your choices and lead to unnecessary stress.

Overpacking:

Don't: Overpack for your honeymoon.

Example: Pack strategically, considering the climate and planned activities, to avoid lugging around unnecessary items.

Ignoring Travel Restrictions:

Don't: Overlook travel restrictions and requirements.

Example: Ensure you have the necessary visas, vaccinations, and documents well in advance.

Overlooking Weather Conditions:

Don't: Disregard the weather conditions of your chosen destination.

Example: Be prepared for varying climates and pack accordingly to enhance your comfort.

Excessive Itinerary:

Don't: Overload your itinerary with too many activities.

Example: Allow for downtime and spontaneous moments to enjoy the honeymoon at a relaxed pace.

Ignoring Health Precautions:

Don't: Neglect health precautions.

Example: Research health guidelines, take necessary vaccinations, and carry a basic medical kit.

Unrealistic Expectations:

Don't: Set unrealistic expectations for your honeymoon.

Example: Understand that not everything may go as planned, and be open to adapting to unforeseen circumstances.

Excessive Screen Time:

Don't: Spend excessive time on electronic devices.

Example: Limit screen time to immerse yourself in the honeymoon experience fully.

Here are some wonderful examples of places to honeymoon...

Australia:

Great Barrier Reef, Queensland:

Explore the vibrant marine life and enjoy secluded island resorts.

Sydney, New South Wales:

Experience the iconic landmarks, vibrant culture, and stunning beaches.

New Zealand:

Queenstown:

Known for its breathtaking landscapes, adventure activities, and serene lakes.

Rotorua:

Immerse yourselves in Maori culture and enjoy geothermal wonders.

Europe:

Santorini, Greece:

Romantic sunsets, white-washed buildings, and crystal-clear waters.

Amalfi Coast, Italy:

Cliffside villages, delicious cuisine, and scenic coastal views.

Asia:

Bali, Indonesia:

Beautiful beaches, lush landscapes, and vibrant culture.

Maldives:

Overwater bungalows, clear turquoise waters, and coral reefs.

Islands:

Bora Bora, French Polynesia:

Luxury overwater bungalows, turquoise lagoons, and romantic sunsets.

Maui, Hawaii, USA:

Diverse landscapes, from volcanic craters to beautiful beaches.

These destinations offer a mix of romance, adventure, and relaxation, making them ideal choices for an unforgettable honeymoon experience.

Australia:

Great Barrier Reef, Queensland:

Explore the vibrant marine life and enjoy secluded island resorts.

Sydney, New South Wales:

Experience the iconic landmarks, vibrant culture, and stunning beaches.

New Zealand:

Queenstown:

Known for its breathtaking landscapes, adventure activities, and serene lakes.

Rotorua:

Immerse yourselves in Maori culture and enjoy geothermal wonders.

Europe:

Santorini, Greece:

Romantic sunsets, white-washed buildings, and crystal-clear waters.

Amalfi Coast, Italy:

Cliffside villages, delicious cuisine, and scenic coastal views.

Asia:

Bali, Indonesia:

Beautiful beaches, lush landscapes, and vibrant culture.

Maldives:

Overwater bungalows, clear turquoise waters, and coral reefs.

Islands:

Bora Bora, French Polynesia:

Luxury overwater bungalows, turquoise lagoons, and romantic sunsets.

Maui, Hawaii, USA:

Diverse landscapes, from volcanic craters to beautiful beaches.

Here are sample honeymoon itineraries for each of the specified destinations to consider:

Asia: Bali, Indonesia

Day 1-3: Arrive in Bali and settle into your luxurious beachfront resort in Seminyak or Nusa Dua. Enjoy relaxing days lounging by the pool, indulging in spa treatments, and exploring the local markets and temples.

Day 4-6: Head to Ubud, the cultural heart of Bali, and immerse yourselves in the lush landscapes, rice terraces, and artisan villages. Visit the Sacred Monkey Forest Sanctuary, Tegalalang Rice Terraces, and Tirta Empul Temple.

Day 7-9: Embark on a romantic getaway to the Gili Islands or Nusa Lembongan for pristine beaches, crystal-clear waters, and world-class snorkeling and diving. Spend your days sunbathing, swimming with turtles, and enjoying candlelit dinners on the beach.

Europe: Santorini, Greece

Day 1-3: Arrive in Santorini and check into your luxury cave hotel overlooking the iconic caldera. Explore the charming villages of Oia, Fira, and Imerovigli, and watch the sunset from a cliffside terrace.

Day 4-6: Discover the volcanic beaches of Santorini, such as Red Beach and Perissa Beach, or take a boat tour to explore the nearby islands of Mykonos and Delos.

Day 7-9: Relax and rejuvenate with wine-tasting tours, cooking classes, and spa experiences. Indulge in traditional Greek cuisine at seaside tavernas and enjoy panoramic views of the Aegean Sea.

Australia: Whitsunday Islands and Great Barrier Reef

Day 1-3: Fly to Hamilton Island and check into your luxury resort overlooking the stunning Whitsunday Islands. Explore the pristine beaches, go snorkeling or diving in the Great Barrier Reef, and take a scenic helicopter flight over Heart Reef.

Day 4-6: Sail on a private yacht or join a day cruise to explore the Whitsunday Islands further, stopping at Whitehaven Beach, Hill Inlet, and secluded coves for snorkeling and swimming.

Day 7-9: Return to Hamilton Island for relaxation and pampering. Enjoy sunset cocktails at One Tree Hill, indulge in gourmet dining experiences, and unwind with couples' spa treatments overlooking the Coral Sea.

USA with Islands: Hawaii

Day 1-3: Arrive in Maui and check into your oceanfront resort in Wailea or Kaanapali. Spend your days exploring Maui's stunning beaches, driving the Road to Hana, and watching the sunrise from the summit of Haleakala.

Day 4-6: Fly to the island of Kauai and immerse yourselves in its natural beauty. Visit Waimea Canyon, take a helicopter tour of the Na Pali Coast, and relax on the secluded beaches of the North Shore.

Day 7-9: Conclude your honeymoon on the island of Hawaii (Big Island) and explore the wonders of Hawaii Volcanoes National Park, snorkel with manta rays at night, and stargaze atop Mauna Kea.

These itineraries offer a blend of relaxation, adventure, and romance, ensuring a memorable honeymoon experience in each destination.

As you prepare for this special time together, remember to savor every moment, embrace new experiences, and celebrate your love in the most magical destinations around the world. Wishing you a honeymoon filled with romance, relaxation, and pure bliss as you begin this exciting chapter of your lives together. Bon voyage and cheers to a lifetime of happiness.

Final note

AS YOU NAVIGATE THE final preparations and details leading up to your special day, take time to breathe, relax, and enjoy the process. Surround yourself with supportive friends and family who can help alleviate any stress and ensure that everything comes together seamlessly. Remember that the true beauty of your wedding lies in the love and commitment you share with your partner, and that is what will shine through on your big day.

From saying "I do" to dancing the night away, may your wedding day be filled with unforgettable moments, laughter, and joy. As you exchange vows and embark on this new chapter together, may your love continue to grow stronger with each passing day. Wishing you a lifetime of happiness, love, and cherished memories as you tie the knot and begin your journey as husband and wife. Cheers to your perfect day and a lifetime of love and happiness ahead!

Thank you for taking the time to read "Tying The Knot: A Stress-Free Guide to Your Perfect Day." If you found the book helpful and enjoyable, I would greatly appreciate it if you could leave a review on Amazon. Your feedback helps other readers discover the book and guides them in their decision-making process. Your support means the world to me, and I'm grateful for your help in spreading the word about my book. Thank you again for your support and for being a part of this journey!

Here are some Post Wedding Tasks to consider:

Thank You Notes and Name Changes

Once the excitement of the wedding day has passed, there are still a few important tasks to attend to as you transition into married life. In this section, we'll discuss two key post-wedding tasks: writing thank-you notes and managing name changes.

Writing Thank-You Notes:

Expressing Gratitude: Take the time to personally thank your guests for their presence, support, and generous gifts. Express your appreciation for their love and well-wishes, and mention specific details about their contribution to your special day.

Timing: Aim to send out thank-you notes within a few weeks of the wedding. While it may feel overwhelming, breaking the task into manageable chunks and setting aside dedicated time each day can help you stay on track.

Personalization: Customize each thank-you note to reflect your relationship with the recipient. Include personal anecdotes, memories, or shared experiences to make each message heartfelt.

Organization: Keep track of gifts received and thank-you notes sent using a spreadsheet or wedding planning app. This will help ensure that no one is inadvertently overlooked and that you can easily track your progress.

Name Changes:

Legal Considerations: If you or your partner plan to change your last name after marriage, research the legal requirements and procedures in your jurisdiction. This may involve obtaining a marriage certificate and updating various forms of identification, such as your driver's license, passport, and social security card.

Notification: Notify relevant parties of your name change, including banks, employers, insurance providers, utility companies, and professional associations. Each organization may have its own process for updating your information, so be prepared to provide documentation as needed.

Patience: Changing your name can be a time-consuming process, so be patient and expect some bureaucratic hurdles along the way. It may take several weeks or even months to complete all necessary updates, but stay organized and persistent to ensure a smooth transition.

Conclusion and Reflections:

As you wrap up the final tasks associated with your wedding, take a moment to reflect on the journey you've embarked upon together. From the excitement of the engagement to the whirlwind of wedding planning and the joy of saying "I do," your wedding marks the beginning of a new chapter in your life.

As you look back on your wedding day, cherish the memories you've created and the love you've shared with family and friends. Celebrate the milestones you've achieved together and the challenges you've overcome as a team. Your wedding is not just a single day but the culmination of your love story, a testament to your commitment to each other, and the foundation upon which you'll build your future together. As you move forward as a married couple, may you continue to support, cherish, and uplift one another through all the highs and lows that life may bring. Remember that your wedding is just the beginning of a lifetime of love, laughter, and adventure, and may your marriage be filled with endless joy, growth, and fulfillment.

Congratulations on your wedding, and here's to a lifetime of happiness together!

Online budgeting Apps and additional digital tools to help plan a wedding

WEDDINGWIRE (WEBSITE and App): Offers comprehensive wedding planning tools including budget management, vendor search, guest list management, and more.

The Knot Wedding Planner (Website and App): Provides a suite of planning tools including budget tracking, vendor recommendations, checklist management, and RSVP tracking.

Zola (Website and App): Features a customizable wedding checklist, budget tracker, guest list manager, and registry tool.

Mint (App): A personal finance app that helps you track expenses, set budget goals, and manage finances leading up to the wedding.

Trello (Website and App): A versatile project management tool that can be customized for wedding planning, allowing you to create boards for tasks, guest lists, vendor contacts, and more.

Google Sheets (Website and App): Create custom wedding planning spreadsheets for budgeting, guest lists, seating arrangements, and other organizational needs.

Evernote (Website and App): An all-in-one note-taking app that can be used to store wedding inspiration, vendor contacts, to-do lists, and other planning details.

WeddingHappy (App): A wedding planning app that generates a personalized wedding timeline and checklist based on your wedding date, helping you stay organized and on track.

Joy (Website and App): Offers a wedding website builder, guest list manager, RSVP tracker, and photo sharing platform, all in one convenient tool.

Honeyfund (Website and App): A honeymoon registry platform that allows couples to create a personalized registry for experiences and activities during their honeymoon.

These digital tools and apps can help streamline the wedding planning process, keep track of expenses, and ensure that every aspect of your special day is well-organized and executed smoothly.

"LOVE IS COMPOSED OF a single soul inhabiting two bodies." - Aristotle.

As you embark on this beautiful journey together, may your love story continue to unfold with grace and joy. Happy wedding planning! Here's to a bright future filled with endless love and happiness!

I hope you find this guide enriching as you navigate through the wonderful journey of wedding planning. May it empower you to create a celebration that reflects your unique love story and brings joy to all who experience it. If you've found value in this guide, sharing your experience through a review would mean the world to us. We would be incredibly grateful Here's to crafting unforgettable moments and a lifetime of happiness together!

With Love

Ange Antony